Candle Making Business

A Beginner's Guide to Starting and Growing
a Home-Based Candle Making Business

By: Doug Yimmer

Contents

Introduction to Candle Making: A Background of the Industry

Candle making and the candle industry have a long history that dates all the way back to 221 BC. Today, candles are predominately used for their fragrance to freshen a home or space. Some people even use them strictly for decoration, without ever lighting them. Thousands of years ago, no one would have thought this would be the outcome of the candle-making industry.

Still, that is not all candles can be used for. Much of the world doesn't realize just how soothing and medicinal a candle can really be. When mixed with all-natural essential oils and soy wax, what is now a candle can double as a massage oil when lit, according to some new modern candle companies.

How did it all begin, though?

Much like other areas of modern life, we can also thank the ancient Romans for candles. They created their hand-dipped tallow candles in 500 BC. Tallow is the rendered fat from animals, like cows and sheep. The Romans obtained this fat and used it for their candles. For the wick, they used an unraveled piece of twine. This was the easiest and most inexpensive way to make candles during this time.

The Romans began using candles for added light in the home, but candles were never their main source of light. Rather, they usually depended on oil lamps for light, the reason being that it was cheaper and easier to obtain olive oil in the Empire than animal fat. You must remember that eating meat during this time period was considered a luxury of sorts. So, they were only able to make candles when they had access to animal meat and therefore fat.

Ancient Rome is often credited for many modern inventions and technologies, but it was ancient China that created the very first candle in 221 BC during the Qin Dynasty. Archaeologists discovered remnants of candles in the now-famous tomb of Qin Shi Huang, who was the first emperor of the Qin Dynasty. The tomb was first discovered in 1974 by farmers in northwest China. Soon after, excavations began. Just last year, archaeologists uncovered even more artifacts from the tomb, which is believed to spread across 38 square miles.

The candle remnants contained whale fat. Given that it was the emperor's tomb, these candles were most likely considered a high luxury during this time as well, especially since they were made of whale fat.

The Fall of the Roman Empire

It was the fall of the Roman Empire in 395 AD that led to the first historic turning point for the candle industry. Olive oil was no longer readily accessible for most people, so the need for quality candles increased tremendously. It was then that the candle industry really formed and took off.

Soon, candlemakers popped up all over the place. Most Europeans knew them as 'chandlers.' They were typically travelers that sold their goods in market stalls, but candles weren't the only thing they made. They produced other items as well, including:

- Soaps
- Sauces
- Vinegar
- Cheeses

Most of these candles were made with tallow wax. Interestingly enough though, when the wax burned, it produced a strong and unpleasant odor. The glycerin in the animal fat was the culprit for this stench. These candles didn't produce much light either, so it didn't take long for chandlers to figure out other methods for making candles.

Beeswax

Chandlers soon discovered they could create candles with beeswax that proved to be much more reliable. It didn't produce an unpleasant odor and even had a brighter light as well. That said, beeswax was even harder to come by than tallow wax, which meant candles of this type were reserved for the upper class. Commoners were left with tallow candles for another five centuries afterward.

The Tipping Point

The 19th century became the tipping point for the candle industry because it marked the first time that candles were made on an industrial scale. This meant that they became a lot cheaper to make, and purchase as well, thanks to a man named Joseph Morgan and his candle-making machine.

This machine truly revolutionized the way candles were made and ensured they would be available to the masses. It utilized a cylinder and a moveable piston. The wax was poured into the machine, and once it solidified, it pushed out the candles and repeated the process over again. It successfully manufactured two tons of candles in just about two hours. That's 3,000 candles!

By this time, paraffin wax became the most popular wax used in candle making. Paraffin wax is made from refining crude petroleum and distilling the residue. The wax produces a high-quality candle with proper lighting and no foul odors. The only drawback is that it has a relatively low melting point, which meant the candles melted extremely fast. This was good news for the candle industry, however, because it meant that people bought them more frequently.

From this point on, the candle industry only continued to grow. By the 1990s, candles with different types of wax became readily available to the masses for the first time.

Today

In today's world, there are many different places to go for your candles. You can choose from any number of mass producers, such as Yankee Candle and Goose Creek. You can also search through a number of private-label companies, like Amy's Country Candles or Seventh Avenue Apothecary, or you can choose from a number of small and local businesses as well.

If you are reading this e-book, chances are, you are interested in the latter. Apps and websites like Etsy and social media platforms have made it easier than ever before to launch and create your own candle-making business.

When you choose to buy from small businesses, there is a higher chance you will receive quality products you can depend on for sustainability, as well as knowing exactly what goes into your candles. Many large companies still use paraffin wax. In the late 1800s, this wax was found to produce chemicals that are harmful to humans once the candle burns. This was reason enough for a lot of people to choose to start buying their candles from small businesses nowadays.

Most small candle businesses add their own flare to their candles as well—a flare you won't get from larger companies. Some businesses choose to add dried herbs and pebbles into their candles, for example.

Simply put, the homemade candle industry is ever-increasing in value. More and more people want to support anything that is sustainably made, especially if it comes from a small or local business. In short, if you are looking to start your own candle-making business, there has never been a better time!

Throughout the entirety of this e-book, you will discover all there is to know about candle making and how to launch your very own candle-making business. Join me as we walk through what it takes to make your own candles on a somewhat large scale and how to thrive as a business owner in today's world. If nothing else, you are sure to learn a great deal about authentic candle making and what it takes to be a small business owner.

Chapter 1: Turning Your Hobby into a Business: A How-To

So you love making candles and think you might want to turn it into a business. At least, that's usually how people find themselves in the candle-making industry in today's world. Typically, if someone feels the urge to start their own business, it's most likely because they enjoy whatever that something is (as a hobby) first. Making the leap from hobby to small business can be and probably is nerve-racking for a number of reasons.

Maybe you are worried about the market and whether or not there's a place for another homemade candle-making business. Maybe you're worried about if you have what it takes to own a business in the first place, or maybe you are worried that if you turn your hobby into a business, you won't love that hobby anymore, and it'll begin to just feel like work instead of a fun release.

Looking at IBIS World findings, the candle industry experienced a decline from 2014 to 2019, but only by 1.5 percent. Although there was a decline, it was very slight and likely won't affect anyone looking to join the industry and start their own small business. Rather, it is the large corporations mass-producing candles that saw more of a decline than small businesses. The world is shifting focus, and more people are attuning to small businesses. So, if you're wondering if there is a place for you and your ideas, there absolutely is. As long as you can find a way to make your business as unique as you are, you won't have any problems paving your way in this industry, and by the end of this e-book, you should know exactly how to do that.

When it comes to recognizing your passions and understanding if you love this hobby enough to still love it after you make it a business—well, that's a mental game you must figure out.

The Mental Game

I have come up with a small mental checklist to help you decide whether or not you have enough passion for turning your hobby into a small business. That said, you must remember that it will take a lot of hard work. When you are trying to turn your hobby into a business, there is a mental shift that has to happen first.

Here are some of the things you should most likely ask yourself before beginning in this venture:

- **Research:** Have you already or are you interested in researching all there is to know about the business side of candle making? It is one thing to have the idea to turn your hobby into a business, but if you aren't willing to put in the research before you begin, then your hobby should probably stay a hobby. Some hobbies are meant to stay hobbies because they bring us peace that other things in life do not. You must be able to look at yourself objectively to figure this out.

- **Other Hobbies:** Bringing me to my next point—are there other hobbies that might work better for you as a business than candle making? The hobby you choose to be your business may or may not be your favorite hobby. Maybe you want to keep your favorite hobby just that, a hobby, for the simple fact that it does bring you peace.

  If you still decide to start a candle-making business, ask yourself if you have other hobbies leftover. No matter what, as humans, we always need some sort of release. If you start this venture in candle making, you will still need a hobby to bring you back down to a peaceful mindset every now and then. Running a business is grueling work, and sometimes it might not seem so fun. It's important to have those releases when you need them.

- **Time:** Lastly, finding the time to begin can seem impossible when working full-time and having a laundry list of other obligations. This is the main reason why starting your own business can be so difficult. You have to come to terms with the fact that most likely, for the first year, you will still be working full-time at another job while you build your small business.

  It typically takes people anywhere from six months to a year to get their business off the ground and be doing it full-time. Sometimes it takes even longer. You will be working 60+ hours a week until that day comes. The days will feel long and exhausting, and maintaining the motivation to continue on might feel tough at times. Still, if you love what you do and you have a real passion for the business, you will succeed against all odds.

Above all else, remember that you can do anything you put your mind to. The mental game is the biggest hurdle to jump when turning your hobby into a business. Yes, starting a business is all-consuming and exhausting but can be one of the most rewarding things you'll ever do if you are willing and able.

If you said yes to all of the things on the checklist above, then a candle-making business quite possibly is the right move for you. However, the last point is so important. I feel the need to reiterate it here.

Don't Quit Your Day Job…Yet!

So many people, when they start their own business, jump the gun and quit their day job to pursue their dreams. Unfortunately, most of us don't have enough savings to support ourselves as we chase our dreams. Even if you have just started your business and made a few sales, it is not time yet to quit your day job.

Rather, look at it as moving in seasons:

- **Season One:** Working full-time at your day job to support your night job of chasing your dreams.
- **Season Two:** Working full-time at your day job and part-time at your dreams.

- **Season Three:** Working part-time at your day job and part-time at your dreams because you now make consistent sales to support this.
- **Season Four:** Working full-time at your dreams because you now make the consistent sales to support this.

These four seasons are vital, and every small business owner goes through them. The importance here is to not jump the gun on any of it. It's incredibly easy to get ahead of yourself and quit your day job before you are really ready to. That's the trick about chasing your dreams. You will likely put all of your passions into chasing those dreams and may even start to dislike or resent your day job.

A healthy mentality is half the battle here. Remember that this day job is supporting you so you can chase those dreams. Love that day job for what it's worth and the fact that it allows you to do such a thing. This will gift you the gratitude necessary to continue on without getting anxious and quitting the job prematurely.

No one likes working 60+ hours a week, and it can seem harder to keep up that schedule when you are so excited to start your new life working your dream job. However, this 60-hour work schedule is actually making you stronger. It is building that mental stamina you will need later on when you begin working for yourself full-time because even though it is your dream job, owning your own business is oftentimes grueling work. There will be many days that you work more than you would like for less pay than you'd like.

Still, all those days will pay off in the end when you have a scalable business with avenues for passive income and an outlook that continues to grow. It might take you ten years to get to that point, but in ten years, you will be happy you did it. Even when the light seems dim, talk yourself into continuing on. You'll be glad you did.

Chapter 2: Things to Know Before You Begin

Arguably the coolest thing about starting your own candle-making business is the fact that you automatically become initiated into a community of like-minded people. Regardless of what you make, starting a business that creates homemade goods puts you in a similar boat with other businesses that make handmade goods. This community is welcoming and pushes one another to succeed.

They all share the same interest in putting out quality and authentic products that can't be found in department or grocery stores. You even open yourself up to other areas of business, including sustainably made clothing, recyclable products, and even small local farms that produce organic foods.

In short, you might own your own business, but you are never alone. There is something comforting about that fact.

When starting your journey down the path of handmade candles, one of the first hurdles to jump is familiarizing yourself with the tools, equipment, cleaning regimens, and different types of candles that are currently offered on the market today. This is where the research begins as well, but luckily, we've mapped all that out for you here.

Let's dive in.

Necessary Equipment and How to Use It

Just like anything else, there are different tools and equipment that every candlemaker uses. Those who have made candles in the past might already have some of the main tools necessary, but as a business, you will probably need a couple of each item. Stocking up on a few of each tool will help you get more orders done quicker. It's also great to have a back-up of everything in the event that something breaks while in the process of making an order.

The great thing about candle making is it doesn't cost an arm and a leg to stock up on the necessities.

Here is a list of the basic tools and supplies needed for candle making:

- Double boiler
- Thermometer
- Measuring instruments
- Handheld butane torch
- Wax
- Wicks
- Molds
- Containers for the candles
- Dyes
- Fragrances
- Additives
- Luster spray
- Packaging materials

The wax, wicks, and fragrances will be talked about in detail in the following chapter. For now, let's dive into the rest of this list.

Double Boiler

If you've ever made a candle, you know how important a good double boiler is. You will need at least one of these to start, but it wouldn't hurt to have a second one by the time your first orders come in. The reason being, that the cleaning process can be a bit lengthy at times. If someone buys two candles in one order, it's more efficient to have a second one on hand. As your business grows, you will most likely end up with a few of these on hand. As you fall into the groove of your workflow, you will come to an understanding of how many double boilers work best for your needs.

To make things even easier on yourself, purchasing a countertop electric burner is also recommended.

Here's a little more info on double boilers for those that are unfamiliar:

In today's world, this is by far the most popular way to heat wax for candle making. Essentially, it works by filling a pot with water and heating it to a slow, rolling boil. You might not even need the water that hot. It just needs to be hot enough to melt the wax. You must also be careful not to burn it.

That said, the entire purpose of a double boiler is to make it nearly impossible to burn the wax.

Once you have the water heating, grab a pot or bowl that sits comfortably at the top of your heated pot. You don't want this bowl necessarily touching the water, but it's okay if it does. It just needs to sit at the top of the pot. Then, you'll place the ideal amount of wax into that top bowl and stir gradually until it's melted.

The idea is that the double boiler provides a slow and even heat to prevent burning the wax. You will also add any dyes, fragrances, and additives into the bowl once the wax has melted completely.

Cleaning

Cleaning the double boiler can be a bit lengthy, but here is a quick and easy step-by-step guide to cleaning your double boiler:

- Once you've finished using it, the wax will most likely be dried up on the sides of the double boilers and any utensils you used in the process of making your candle.
- Go ahead and stick that double boiler back into the base pot and reheat all the wax. You'll want to throw all other utensils into the double boiler as well.
- After a few minutes, the wax will be all melted down to the bottom of the double boiler.
- Take out your utensils and wipe them clean with a paper towel.
- Then, pour out any excess wax that's in the double boiler into a disposable cup or container. Once the wax is dried, you can safely throw it away.

- You can now wipe down the double boiler with a paper towel like you did the utensils.

It's important to note that you never want to pour hot wax down your drain because it will harden and clog your piping system. Always throw it away after it has had time to cool down first in a disposable cup.

Once the double boiler has been wiped down, you might want to repeat the process to ensure you removed all of the excess fragrances, so they don't contaminate your next candle. At this point, you can rinse the double boiler with soapy water if you feel so inclined, but only after all the wax has been properly removed.

Thermometer

A thermometer is a must-have for candle making and can be considered one of the utensils mentioned in the section above. If you read different online forums, you might find that some people believe a thermometer isn't necessary for candle making. Many people say that wax melts at 200 degrees, and once it melts, there really is no use for the thermometer.

However, this couldn't be further from the truth. Aside from the double boiler, the thermometer is without a doubt the most important utensil used in candle making. It is absolutely vital to know what temperature the wax is at once you've melted it, the temperature at the moment you pour, and the cooling temperature. If you aren't aware of the temperature at every stage of the candle-making process, you will likely run into cracks and tunnels within the candle. Basically, disaster would ensue.

There might be some experts out there that have made candles for decades and can seemingly "eyeball" the temperature, but as a beginner in the industry, this is most certainly not ideal. It can even be dangerous.

Here are the ideal temperatures to remember for each stage of candle making:

- **Boiling Point:** Heat to 185 degrees Fahrenheit before adding fragrances and dyes.
- **Pouring Point:** Temperature must be between 140–160 degrees Fahrenheit to ensure no cracking or tunnels happen.
- **Cooling Point:** Never try to accelerate cooling. Allow the candle to cool naturally. Wick will need to be held sturdily in place until the candle solidifies.

Temperature is also crucial if you are using molds to create your candles rather than containers. This will be talked about more in the sections below.

Cleaning

The thermometer will undoubtedly be covered in wax after each use. The best way to clean this utensil is to wipe it off after each time you dip it into the wax. However, if the wax hardens on the thermometer before you get the chance to wipe it clean, you can place it in the double boiler, as mentioned in the section above.

Measuring Instruments

Measuring instruments are also extremely important in candle making because different candles require different amounts of wax. If you add fragrances and other additives, you will need to be aware of how much fragrance to add based on how much wax you are using. Typically, most people use one ounce of fragrance for every pound of wax used.

Most double boilers come with a measuring line built in to the inside of the pot. This makes it easier for you to see just how much wax you have added. If you are new to candle making, it's always best to add more wax than you think you'll need. You will also need a scale that measures in ounces out to the 100th decimal place.

How to use these instruments:

- First, you will get your scale. It is recommended to add a paper plate on top to catch any messes and to protect the scale from the hot pot.
- Then, grab your pot of freshly melted wax and dye, and place it on the plate.
- Tare the scale-out to zero.
- Now, you can add one ounce of fragrance to every pound of melted wax.
- Stir in the fragrance for about two or three minutes as it cools before pouring the mixture into your candle container. Stirring for this long helps to bind the fragrance to the wax.
- If you stop stirring and you can see the fragrance oil sitting on top, keep stirring!

This is by far the easiest and most precise way to add in the fragrance. Otherwise, you may add too little or too much fragrance and mess up all of your hard work.

Handheld Butane Torch

A handheld and refillable butane torch isn't a necessity, but is always nice to have. If you've ever worked with candles, you know that once that wax starts to cool, it cools quickly. This can lead to some mistakes with your candle if you aren't ready. A handheld torch is a great way to precisely apply heat to a given area and help the wax melt again, and rather quickly at that.

Handheld torches come in handy specifically for those candles created in molds. Sometimes, especially when first starting out, working with molds is tough. There will most likely be areas on the candle that aren't even or get stuck in the mold. If you don't have a torch, these candles could be rendered useless. However, with the torch, you can quickly apply heat and get that candle looking the way it's meant to.

It needs to be noted that this particular skill is a bit more advanced. You are working with an open flame and essentially handcrafting your candle to customize the shape. You may not want to purchase this just yet if you've never worked with torches or candles in the past. That said, once you hone in on your skill set, this is a great tool to help you create designs in your candles if you choose to do so.

If that is the case, you may also want to look into purchasing a set of carving utensils. Owning a set of carving tools can really help you discover your niche and create candles that are unique to you. This could also help you with branding and sales later down the line. Still, starting a business is a lot of work in and of itself, so if you've never worked with carving tools before, you may save this for a later date.

Molds

As mentioned in the thermometer section, molds are another fun way to create candles. Molds are made from silicone and can be purchased easily online. If you would like to customize your own molds, you will need to find a supplier to do so.

To start, purchasing one mold will do until you are comfortable with them. They are relatively easy to work with. However, the temperature plays a crucial role in how well your candles will turn out when placed into a mold.

First and foremost, you must always make sure your mold is clean. The best way to clean most of the wax out of the mold is to place it upside down on a baking sheet in your oven and set the oven to broil. Within five minutes the wax should be melted, and you can wipe the mold clean with a paper towel. Again, it is preferred that you do not clean your molds in the sink as this could lead to clogging up the plumbing system.

Then, when the wax for your candles is cool enough to pour, you can pour them straight into the mold as you would a regular candle container.

It is absolutely vital that the candle cools for several hours before you remove it from the mold. You are cautioned not to accelerate cooling in any way as this could lead to damage to the candle. Once the candle cools for four hours or more, depending on the size, you can then remove it from the mold. A silicone mold makes removal quite easy if the entire process was done correctly. Still, working with molds is tough and will most likely take you a few dozen mess-ups before you nail the perfect molded candle.

Candle Containers

The great thing about candle making and starting your own business is the versatility in what kind of candle containers you want to use. The options are essentially endless, but here are a few examples of what other candlemakers have used in the past:

- 4 oz. metal tin containers
- Clear glass containers in various sizes
- Stained glass containers in various sizes
- Frosted glass containers in various sizes
- Tealights
- Ceramic bowls and jars in various sizes
- Coconut shells

You can even look for containers that are oddly shaped, like hexagon, triangle, or round containers. The great thing about candles is that the liquid wax can be poured into almost anything.

Your choice of candle container could be the main branding point for your business. Maybe you are known for putting your candles in quirky containers that are unique and one-of-a-kind.

This could be something your customers grow to love about your business.

It is best to start with more widely used containers, though, like metal tins and glass jars. Once you get a feel for candle making, start experimenting with different options!

You can never have too many containers in this business. You can expect some will break and be unusable as well. That said, a great place to start is with a few metal tins and a few glass containers to get the ball rolling.

Still, it should be noted that safety is a concern when choosing your candle containers. Different tests will need to be done before you can safely place a new candle container for sale on your website or in your shop. The last thing you want is a liability on your hands. This will be discussed more in Chapter 10.

Packaging Materials

Packaging materials and labeling will be touched on more in-depth in Chapter 9 but should also be mentioned here because it is technically a material that is needed for a candle-making business. There are many different hoops one must jump through when figuring out what packaging material works best for your products and how to find the right packaging at the right price.

In terms of how much to have on hand, this also depends on the supplier you choose to go with. That said, it is recommended to begin this search right away because it could take a while to find a suitable supplier. You will also want to begin working on the design process so when you do find a supplier, you have your design ready and can order the packaging right away. It is best to order one (most likely bulk) order of packaging to begin with. Even if you find yourself sitting on this packaging material for a while before making sales, you will need to have it on hand.

Once your business launches, you never know when your first sale will be. So, it's always best to have the materials ready to go when the time comes.

Here are some things to think about when it comes to packaging materials:

- **Affordability:** Especially when first starting out, affordability is everything.
- **Safety:** Candles are fragile. It's important to have packaging that reflects that fragility.
- **Size:** Chances are, you will create multiple different candle types that are different sizes. It's important to go with a supplier that can keep up with these different sizing options.
- **Sustainability:** More and more people are buying from sustainable companies. If sustainability is important to you, then the packaging will also need to reflect this.
- **Design:** As mentioned, you will most likely want to put your branding on the packaging as well. Going with a supplier that allows you to fully customize your packaging at a great price is ideal.

Thankfully, it doesn't take a lot of big and expensive equipment to start your own candle-making business. Just a few essential tools that you might want to stock up on. As your business progresses, you will modify this list to suit your needs.

That said, every candlemaker needs to know the ins and outs of candle wax, wicks, dyes, fragrances, and other additives. It's always good to stock up on these things because you can never have enough. In the next chapter, we will discuss everything there is to know about different candles throughout history and the products you can use to make your candles stand out.

Chapter 3: Knowing Your Candles

Now that we have covered the tools and other supplies necessary for starting a candle business, let's move on to the candles themselves. As you well know, candles have an extensive history, and the market for them only seems to continue to grow. But we haven't talked about all the different types of candles the world has seen.

Learning about the history of the different types of candles will hopefully spark some creativity within you for branding. It will also give you a little insight as to what worked and what didn't work in the past.

The Different Candle Styles Throughout History

This might come as a surprise, but some of the first candles in history were essentially miniature torches. It makes sense though; before candles, torches were the closest thing to a portable flame. Oil lamps were also popular during this time but had a slightly different design. The history is unclear, but seemingly the ancient Egyptians, Romans, and Chinese are all thought to have done the same thing. They dipped the core of a reed into animal fat and placed it on a miniature torch-like post.

It didn't take long for candle technology to advance in the Roman Empire. They soon developed a candle that came with its very own wick—the first of its kind. By contrast, they used rolled papyrus and dipped it in melted beeswax or tallow. They repeated this process a few times to build more layers and make the candle thicker. The Chinese, on the other hand, used rolled rice paper for the wick in their candles and dipped them in whale fat or wax from insects and seeds. They even used paper tubes to shape and mold the candle.

The shape and style of candles didn't really change from this time until the 1830s with the invention of Joseph Morgan's candle-making machine. His machine produced thousands of small cylinder candles in an incredibly short time.

Today, there are countless ways to make candles. You can pour the wax into nearly any type of container and make an excellent quality candle. That said, there are a few different types or categories of candles on the market. Most candle business owners will follow one or more of the following candle types:

- **Flameless:** There are flameless, artificial candles. To any candlemaker, this type of candle might seem like a joke, but they are still called candles!
- **Utility Candles:** This type of candle serves a particular purpose and isn't meant for decoration or to freshen up a space. Insect repellent candles are a good example of this type of candle.
- **Birthday Candles:** This type might also seem silly, but if we are talking about candles, you have to mention birthday candles! They come in all sizes and shapes. You can even find some in the shape of numbers, letters, and whole words.
- **Tealights:** These are most likely the smallest candles you'll see, and they are usually put into other things to provide light (jack-o-lanterns) or heat (wax melts).

- **Votive:** This type of candle is usually cylindrical in shape and not in a container. They are slightly bigger than tealights and do not produce any smoke.
- **Taper:** The taper candle is reminiscent of the beginning days of candles. They are tall, skinny, and cylindrical in shape. More often than not, they are used for decoration. Sometimes they are still used in religious ceremonies and birthday celebrations.
- **Container Candle:** Any candle that is in a container falls in this category, whether the container is metal, glass, ceramic, or anything else. Most candles of this type are functional in some way. Maybe they are known for their fragrance and freshening up an area. You will rarely see a container candle used only for decoration.
- **Massage Candles:** Massage candles are technically container candles, but they are unique in nature. The wax for the candle doubles as a massage oil and is dripped directly onto the skin. These candles are soothing and meant specifically for relaxation. They often are filled with calming and relaxing fragrances.
- **Pillar:** Pillar candles are tall, wide cylinders, which is where they get their name from. Most of the time, this type of candle is used strictly for decoration. Sometimes they have fragrances, but most of the time they don't. There is also a giant version of this type of candle. Giant pillar candles are usually scented and have three wicks in them. When burned, the wax melts down the side, so it's often recommended that these candles be placed on a plate if you plan to burn them.
- **Carved Pillar:** This could technically be a subgroup of the pillar candles, but some people carve their pillar

candles. This is a unique style of candle making and shows incredible craftsmanship. Candles of this nature are usually more expensive.

- **Floating:** If you want to add atmosphere to the room or event, then floating candles are your best bet. As the name suggests, this type of candle can actually float in a cup of water while lit. The main advantage to floating candles is the fact that you don't have to worry about melted wax dripping down the sides of anything. These candles are typically very small as well and mainly used as a decorative lighting centerpiece or another type of décor.
- **Made in a Mold:** Most molds are made from silicone, so it is easier to work with this type of candle. If you've just started with carving your candles but haven't quite mastered the technique enough to sell, you can achieve a similar effect with mold candles. As mentioned in a previous chapter, you can have a custom mold made to create any shaped candle you like. The only downside is that these candles are usually smaller.

Reading about all the different types of candles might feel overwhelming right now, especially if you haven't decided what route you want to take your business. Use this list, rather, as inspiration to create candles of your own.

If you plan on starting your own business, you will most likely only start with one or maybe a few different types of candles. Hardly anyone that makes candles will offer every single type in their shop - that is, unless it is a larger corporation. Smaller business owners usually stick to one type of candle and master it in their own unique way.

You can't stop there, though. It is—of course—important to find a way to stand out from the crowd. By all means, customizing your own candle style is a great way to do this. However, one must also have quality ingredients (so to speak) in their candles. A major ingredient, and perhaps the most important, is the wax.

Traditional Wax Types

At the very beginning of the days of candle making, chandlers really only had animal fat to work with. This didn't leave very many options to choose from. Later, the world finally started to see a few variations in wax types, such as:

- Insect and seed wax
- Beeswax
- Tallow wax
- Bleached spermaceti wax
- Paraffin wax
- Soybean wax

The great thing about the candle industry is that even in today's world, you still have all of these options for wax. You can even use animal fat wax if you'd like. Most people don't, however. In this day and age, animal fat wax is harder to come by than any other type of wax.

Here are some of the other types of wax that are available today but weren't available a few years ago:

- Palm wax
- Bayberry wax

- Liquid wax

Insect and Seed Wax

This type of wax is rarely ever used today, but it's worth a mention because you might decide to make your own version of wax for your candles. This is an ambitious feat but can really help your business stand out. Ancient China coined the use of this type of wax, and it was used as a way to produce candles without the horrible odor of animal fat.

Beeswax

Beeswax is extremely old. It has been used to make candles for centuries now. It is tried and true, which is why most people still rely on it for their candles. They know this type of wax works, so why change it? This type of wax also has a few benefits that stand out aside from how long it's been used. Candles made from beeswax can actually help improve the air quality by reducing pollutants in the air.

Because of all the benefits, this wax is usually sold at a higher price point. This is something to keep in mind when searching for the perfect wax for your candles.

Tallow Wax

Tallow wax is also an extremely old technique. It was mainly used centuries ago but is sometimes still used today. Tallow is the rendered fat from animals. It is great for sturdy candles, especially if the fat comes from cows or sheep. However, this type of wax can produce an unpleasant odor for this reason. Added fragrances might get covered up by the smell of fat.

Bleached Spermaceti Wax

This type of wax increased in popularity in the 18th century, in tandem with the industrial growth of whaling. Just as it sounds, this type of wax is derived from the sperm of whales. It was yellow in nature, so they usually bleached it to make it more translucent like other waxes on the market. It also didn't produce an odor like other waxes during that time.

However, using this type of wax isn't advised in today's world, as whaling is now illegal in most countries.

Paraffin Wax

Paraffin is now the most common wax used by large corporations in candle making. It is derived from petroleum and has a high melting point. Larger corporations favor this type of wax because its rigidity ensures the candles won't easily break and that they last longer than most other candles.

However, this type of wax releases chemicals into the air when burning the candle. For this reason, most small businesses shy away from paraffin.

Soybean Wax

Soybean wax only seems to grow in popularity. Once word got around that soy wax doesn't have petrol-carbon soot or any other pollutants when burned, popularity seemed to grow rather quickly. It also is a durable wax and lasts about 40% longer than many other types of wax, including paraffin.

The only downside to soy wax is the price point. You will most likely have to raise the price of your candles if you use this type of wax.

Palm Wax

Palm wax is much thicker than most other wax, meaning it is long-lasting as well. A long burn time is something that customers tend to look for in a candle. For this reason, palm wax might be a good option for you. It is made by placing palm oil under extremely high temperatures and pressure. Then, the fatty acids are separated and used to make the wax.

This type of wax is also biodegradable, making it eco-friendly.

Bayberry Wax

Bayberry wax hasn't grown in popularity as fast as soy wax did, but it is definitely on the rise for being the next great eco-friendly wax. It is a plant-based wax, made from picking lots of bayberries and boiling them down. They're then filtered through cheesecloth for their wax.

This wax has a downside as well. It isn't as durable as other waxes because it is plant-based. Because of this, many people decide to cut their wax mixture. They will use half bayberry wax and half of another wax, like beeswax, to make their candles a little sturdier.

Liquid Wax

Liquid wax is made with different kinds of oils, so it maintains a liquid state and never hardens. This type of wax is ideal because it doesn't produce any smoke or soot. That also means it is better for the air quality, which is why these candles are great for a home or office space. You also won't ever have to deal with cleaning wax drippings from anything because it is always contained in its container.

The downside to this type of wax is that you might feel like your creativity is stifled because you can't shape or mold the wax. That said, if you have beautiful containers you want to showcase, this is a great way to do that.

It may take a few tries to find the right wax for your business. The wax you choose for your business might not be the wax you use when making candles as a hobby. It is important to allow yourself the courtesy of playing with all different types of wax. Try to find every wax listed above and see which works best for your needs.

You might find one that surprises you!

Traditional Wick Types

The candle wick is the single most important part of the candle. Without it, the candle is rendered useless. You may have thought you were done with the major decisions after you chose your type of candles and wax, but the decisions have only just begun. However, it is best to choose the type of wax you'll use before the type of wicks.

Why is this?

Two words: burning rate.

The wick has its own burning rate, and when it's paired with a certain wax, it could burn a lot faster than when paired with another type of wax. Without a helpful guide, you could be stuck doing hours of guess and check work, spending hundreds of dollars just to test which wicks work the best for your needs.

Fortunately, the information below should give you everything you need to know to make an informed decision:

Different Type of Wicks and How to Choose the Right One for You

First and foremost, it's important to understand the job of a wick. Its purpose is to deliver the fuel (wax) to the flame of the candle. It is essentially a fuel pump that initiates the entire process of igniting the flame and keeping it ablaze. There are many different types of wicks in today's world, but traditionally, they've always been twisted or braided fibers. It is the twisted action that helps the wax travel up toward the flame.

Depending on the wax and wick friendship, some wicks might draw in more wax than others, and vice versa.

The twisted or braided wick is known as the traditional style of wick but most certainly was not the first wick the world knew. As mentioned in previous sections, ancient Rome,

Egypt, and China all had their own versions of candles with their own versions of wicks. The Chinese used rice paper for their wicks. The Romans utilized papyrus for their wicks by rolling it up and dipping it into the wax, while the ancient Egyptians used the core of reeds for their wicks.

These are all still perfectly viable options for wicks in today's world, but you won't see much of them anymore. The candle industry has evolved past the use of these medieval wicks. It is now easier to find several other style wicks than any of the three types used in ancient times.

In today's world, there is a near-endless list of wick types. They come in all different shapes, sizes, materials, colors, and even fragrances.

Here are some of the different factors to keep in mind when choosing the wicks that are right for you:

- The wax you decide to go with and how it reacts with different wicks
- The melting point of the wax
- The type of candle
- The size of the candle
- The candle's shape
- Dyes and fragrances you plan to use

Not only does the size of the candle matter, but the size of the wick matters as well. The bigger the wick, the more wax it will consume. Contrarily, if the wick is too small relative to the amount of wax used in the candle, the wick won't get enough oxygen, and the flame won't stay ignited.

Wick Style

As mentioned above, most wicks are either twisted or braided in today's world. Believe it or not, there's a major difference between these two styles. If you would like higher quality candles at a higher price point, go with braided wicks. They seem to produce a slow, consistent burn no matter what. Twisted wicks, on the other hand, burn faster, and the wick can begin to open and fray. Birthday candles are a good example of twisted wick candles.

Keeping these things in mind, here's a closer look at some of the most popular wicks on the market today:

Flat Wicks

Flat cotton wicks are a very traditional style of wick. One could say they self-maintain because of the tip of the wick, which curls into itself. This type of wick is similar to square wicks, but they aren't as thick as the latter. They are either knitted or flat-braided with three pieces of fiber. They burn consistently and are commonly used in taper or pillar candles. They work best with a taller, skinnier type of candle. The best wax for this type of wick is soy wax.

Square Wicks

Square wicks are bleached cotton wicks. Usually braided or knitted, they are thicker than other wicks. They are also designed to bend at the tip. This is a great feature to have because it creates a sizeable ember at the tip of the wick. This ember radiates heat to the outer edges of the candle, so the candle burns more evenly.

This type of wick works best with soy, palm, paraffin, or beeswax. Nearly any wax on the market today will produce excellent burning effects with this wick. It also works great with multiple different types of candles, including pillar, molded, and dipping taper candles.

Cored Wicks

Cored wicks can be braided or knitted. They are popular because of the added core material that keeps the wick straight while burning. A cored wick will usually come in one of three material variations:

- Cotton
- Zinc
- Paper

The great thing about cored wicks is their versatility. They can be used in nearly any wax and for any type of candle. They work best in container candles, votives, and pillars. There is a noteworthy tip for those that haven't worked with cored wicks before - it is recommended that you pre-wax the wicks and let them dry before placing them in the candle. This will strengthen the rigidity of the candle overall.

HTP Wicks

HTP wicks are a common choice because they have a nice list of benefits that other wicks don't provide. Firstly, they are self-trimming. This means little to no maintenance, which is exactly what customers are looking for in a candle. Secondly, they are, in fact, coreless wicks but provide the same rigidity as a core style wick. Third, they produce less carbon heading than most other wicks, including core wicks. Lastly, they have an improved wax pool symmetry. In other words, they burn evenly and consistently.

These are all things customers look for in their candles. If you want to work with this wick, you are best off using either palm, soy, or paraffin wax.

Performa Coreless Wicks

As stated in the name, Performa Coreless wicks are coreless and are flat, braided wicks. The coolest thing about this type of wick is the fact that it stands straight no matter what. If you choose to work with this type of wick, you will want to use either palm, soy, or paraffin wax.

LX Wicks

LX wicks are excellent, stable, and consistent wicks. They work best with container and pillar candles. The type of wax it prefers is paraffin or soy. These are the two waxes that are more rigid than their competitors and LX wicks like that. This type of wick also features a braid style, but in its own unique way. These wicks are coreless but also flat braided. They are manufactured with stabilizing threads that make sure to provide an optimum burn. They also reduce smoke and soot when the flame is extinguished for better air quality in the home.

RRD Series Wicks

RRD wicks are cotton-cored wicks. They feature a round braided style to provide increased fuel flow. In other words, these wicks tend to burn faster than some other wicks, regardless of the wax. It is still a great option for candles, though. It provides a consistent and stable flame. If you do decide to go with this wick, you might want to look into purchasing palm wax to go with it. This is the type of wax it works with the best. It's also good for any type of candle or candle container.

CD Series Wicks

This type of wick works best with paraffin and soy wax. It likes those hard to melt waxes. CD wicks are inherently coreless and have a flat braided style. This is one of your higher-quality cotton wicks. It will come accompanied with a paper filament woven within and around it. Those that use this type of wick find that it promotes maximum consistency in the burning department, especially if you use paraffin or soy wax.

Wooden Wicks

Wooden wicks are some of the newest types of wicks on the market. You can buy them in either hardwood or softwood. If you prefer the sweet sound of crackling wood with your candles, then softwood wicks are the way to go. Wooden wicks also tend to be a little less maintenance than the other options listed above. They tend to burn slow no matter what kind of wax you use.

There are two possible downsides to this type of wick, though. They are a natural product, so sometimes they have dark spots in the wood. This can disrupt the usual performance of the wick. It doesn't make the candle dangerous, per se, but can cause the flame to extinguish itself. One can easily wait for the wick to cool off and break off the burnt part once it reaches the top of the wick, or they can let it burn through. Another possible downside is the fact that this type of wick is a lot more expensive than others on the market, mainly because it is a natural product.

Regardless of your needs, there is a type of wick out there that is right for you. It might take a couple of practice candles before you find the magic combination you are looking for, but that's the fun of candle making! Remember to have fun with your candles. Yes, you are trying to start a business, but choosing these fundamental items tends to be the most fun part of setting up said business.

Not only that, but remember that once you pick a certain combo, you aren't stuck with it forever. It is your business, after all. If you decide later that you want to change things up, do it!

Before we move on to the next subject at hand, let's talk about a couple of bonus decisions that you will most likely have to make:

- The different fragrances and other additives you plan to add to your candles
- Luster spray

Learning About Fragrances and Other Additives

In the beginning days of candle making, it wasn't customary for chandlers to put any fragrances or additives into their candles. They simply dipped them in the wax they had on hand, and that was that. In today's world, candles are utilized more for comfort and decoration than for purpose and functionality. That said, there are a few different additives on the market that larger companies use for their candles. These additives make the candle's scent last longer than candles without additives.

There are natural and artificial additives, and they are usually for sale anywhere online. Here are three common additives used today:

Stearic Acid

Stearic acid is an additive derived from vegetables or tallow. Small business owners that want long-lasting scented candles without artificial chemicals might choose this type of additive. The scent isn't the only area where stearic acid can benefit the candle. It is also used to provide a glossy finish and to help retain color and sturdiness.

This additive usually comes in powder form and works the best in soy wax candles. This is yet another reason small candle business owners love it. Most small business owners want to be as sustainable and eco-friendly as possible, and this is an epic combination if that is your main goal. If you use soy wax and plant-based stearic acid, you can technically even sell your candles as vegan-friendly products.

It also works well with paraffin wax, but using this type of wax means the candle is no longer vegan-friendly. Still, the best ratio of stearic acid to wax – regardless of the wax – is 10% to 90%.

Vybar

Vybar, on the other hand, is a synthetic compound. This compound is made strictly to help the scent last longer in a candle. Not only does the scent last longer, but it gives you the opportunity to have more fragrance to your candle from the start. The rule of thumb is to add one ounce of fragrance for every pound of wax, but Vybar allows you to add up to half an ounce more.

You can also buy this substance in three different forms, all of which depend on the type of wax you go with for your business:

- **Vybar 103:** This type is mainly used for candle molds. It has the highest melting point of all three options.
- **Vybar 260:** This type is mainly used for container candles because it has a lower melting point.
- **Vybar 343:** This type is mainly used in mottled candles because of the color vibrancy it leaves on finished candles.

Yes, Vybar is made strictly for enhancing the scent of candles, but it also helps produce vibrant colors for your candles. This is a nice added bonus because sometimes dyes by themselves don't cut it.

Beeswax Pellets

The great thing about beeswax pellets is that they can be used on their own. However, you can also add them to paraffin or soy wax. If you choose to go this route, only add about 10% of the beeswax pellets to the other wax. These pellets are actually a type of wax, so it's okay if you add more than you originally intended. This will also help increase the burn time and color vibrancy, along with extending the life of the fragrance.

Beeswax pellets give you the advantage of having the beeswax scent without the cost of buying pure beeswax. It really brings out the scent of honey and almond fragrances. Beeswax pellets are one of the more natural additives for candles. Perhaps the greatest benefit of this type of additive is that you can get extra long-lasting scents without adding extra oils. The fragrances come straight from the wax itself. That's also why it works best with more natural scents.

These are the three main additives people tend to rely on for their candles, but they are by no means the only additives out there. You can even use Crisco shortening as an additive.

Now, let's take a deep dive into the world of fragrances!

All About the Different Types of Fragrances in Candle Making

In the early days of candle making, candles weren't scented. Candles were seen as more of a functional component, like a torch or lamp. These days, it's hard to walk past a candle without picking it up and taking a nice whiff. When it comes to fragrances in candle making, they are one of the most defining characteristics, and the possibilities are essentially endless.

A fragrance has the ability to pull at heartstrings like nothing else. The brain is the main reason for the emotional response one receives when they smell a certain scent they either love or hate. When smelling a scent, the brain makes a memory of it by triggering a specific emotion. In turn, the fragrances you choose for your candles are important because they have the possibility to help create amazing memories for years to come…

—but no pressure.

Seriously, if you follow the tips below, you shouldn't have any problems choosing fragrances and even creating new ways to scent a candle.

Tip 1: Consider Your Niche

The world of fragrances can feel overwhelming at first. The pressure to make the perfect candles that express your branding while still smelling like something people want to buy is nerve-racking, to say the least. Then you have to pile on a seemingly endless list of fragrance oils and different ways to scent a candle, which can make the choices nearly impossible.

Before you even dive down the rabbit hole of fragrances, head back to the drawing board. Refresh your memory with what exactly your niche is (if you don't have a niche yet, don't worry, we will talk about this later). Branding is everything, and your candle scents have a lot to say about your branding.

Refreshing your memory can help you answer some of these main questions:

What is the purpose of my candles?

What direction do you want to take your business? Your candle purpose will reflect this. Believe it or not, every candle has a purpose. Most homemade candle businesses create candles for the ambiance effect. This is the most general or overarching type of candle; most candles in the home fall under this type.

However, there are other types that work great for the home as well. Some candles are odor-neutralizers, which work phenomenally in any home. Everyone suffers from unappealing odors plaguing the home from time to time. An odor-neutralizer candle brings back that pop of freshness while eliminating bad odors.

There are other candlemakers that make their candles specifically for giving massages. The wax is mixed with oil, and when it melts, it is poured onto the skin for the perfect, sensual massage experience. The fragrances in this type of candle are usually either relaxing, fresh, or even fragrant-less!

Of course, you may decide to have a few different types of candles offered in your business, but it's important to focus on getting one really good product to start with.

Where will they be placed?

When it comes down to it, it's hard to predict where the customer will place the candle once they purchase. The type of candle you decide to go with should give you some insight, but you never really know what the customer plans to do with the candle. Because of this, it is always a great idea to include in the product description something about the ideal environment for the particular candle.

The reason being, some spaces are better suited for certain fragrances. The product description is a great place to give them ideas of spaces the candle will succeed, but they are free to make their own decision in the end. A good rule of thumb is to consider the candle being placed in a living or bedroom. Keeping this in mind will help you further decide what scents will work best.

Are you looking for strong scents or subtlety?

To continue, the ideal placement of the candle will also reveal how strong to make the scent. You never want the candle to seem overwhelming, but you also don't want it to seem fragrant-less. Finding that fine line is tough and might take a couple of practice candles to nail, but a lot of it has to do with the type of scents you pick out in the first place.

For example, it is usually best to go with fresh-smelling candles in the bathroom, while people usually choose woody smells for their living room. That said, there are some fresh and woody smells that are subtle, while others are strong and even overbearing. You must play around with the different fragrances to see what combinations work best for you and your candles.

Tip 2: Narrow the Search by Choosing a Type of Fragrance

Now you are ready to begin searching through the different types of fragrances. Although not by much, this will still help you narrow down your search. Throughout history, candles saw many different fragrant evolutions, from no fragrance and wax with poor odors to better-smelling wax still without fragrance to candles with a small variety of different basic fragrances. Now, it's as if the world continues to test the limits of what constitutes not only a candle, but the fragrance engulfed within it.

The latest trend in candle fragrances and candle making, in general, is to only use natural, sustainably made and resourced fragrances. Candlemakers that choose this route tend to spend a little more overall. Therefore, their candles are more expensive as well. Still, do not let this deter you from pursuing this route. It is one that benefits the environment. People will pay extra to know exactly how products are made and what their impact on the earth is.

That said, people also continue to test the boundaries of what makes something a fragrance. This list is meant to give you some examples of the different ways people have scented their candles in the past. By all means, have the courage to go your own route with it. This is your creativity's time to shine!

Here is a list of things people have used in the past to scent their candles:

Standard or Natural Fragrance Oils

Standard and natural fragrance oils are the traditional methods now used to scent candles. Nearly every large candle-making company today uses standard fragrance oils, which is another area of business ethics that come into play. Standard fragrance oils are known to have chemicals in them like phthalate and parabens. Natural fragrances are free of these chemicals, but they can sometimes cost seven times as much as the standard fragrance oils.

The difference between standard/natural fragrance oils and essential oils is that fragrance oils are typically made up of essential oils and some other natural element. Because of this, fragrance oils usually give off a stronger scent.

Pure Essential Oils

The keyword here is pure. If you choose to go with essential oils, it is best to source them from a company you can trust to always provide 100% pure natural oils. The essential oils that grocery stores and convenience stores have on their shelves are equivalent to purchasing standard fragrance oils. Yes, they are cheaper, but they are filled with chemicals that nobody desires.

One hundred percent pure essential oils are one of the best things you can use to scent your candles. Companies like Young Living have a Seed to Seal guarantee. This means that they plant the herb themselves and grow it, harvest it, and transform it into the oil you order from their site. When you order from a company with ethics such as these, you can rest assured that your candles aren't harmful to breathe when burned.

Dried Herbs

Using dried herbs isn't necessarily a new concept, but it is one that doesn't get adopted by many. It should also be noted that candlemakers who do utilize fresh and dried herbs and flowers will also use some other type of fragrance. Simply put, fresh and dried herbs and flowers don't carry the same volume that essential oils and natural fragrance oils do.

Dried herbs also make for a nice visual aspect to the candle. The safest use of dried or fresh herbs and flowers is to add them to the wax during the heating process. Once the wax melts, add in the flowers or herbs and stir for a couple more minutes. The herbs will be coated in wax—inside the candle—which will keep them from catching on fire. Still, there are some people who like to dress the top of the candle as well. They might decorate the candle with dried herbs and flowers as well as crystals and other small things. That said, you have to be careful with how many dried herbs you place on top of the candle because this can be a fire hazard.

These aren't the only ways to scent a candle, either. I have seen a candle with a slice of an orange at the bottom of it. The way you choose to scent your candle might look different depending on your niche. Maybe you are known for using as many real scents from nature as possible.

Tip 3: Complete the Search by Choosing a Scent Category

Once you've narrowed down which type of fragrance(s) you want to use for your candles, you can then move on to choosing a scent category. There are thousands of different scents one can create in today's world, but each scent can be placed into a category. All scents in a particular category will have the same general components and inherent smell.

There are four primary scent categories:

- Floral
- Woody
- Fresh
- Exotic

Of course, there are holiday-inspired candles as well that can be placed into their own "seasonal" category. They are usually a mix of the above-stated categories. It's also worth noting that your candle doesn't have to stick to just one scent category. Oftentimes, people will recommend that you only stick to one category per candle, but at the end of the day, it is your business, and if you want to create a combination scent, that is up to you.

It isn't an uncommon occurrence for this to happen, anyway. For instance, woody and floral scents go great together as well as floral and fresh scents. Woody and exotic scents work well together as well.

Below is a short description of each scent category:

Floral

This category is more obvious than the others, but it contains scents derived from flowers. Whether the scents are natural or artificial, all flower scents are found here. Since the time of the ancient civilizations, florals have been used not only for personal fragrances and perfumes but to clean and mask odors, especially during funerals.

Floral scents are usually synonymous with calming and relaxation as well as romantic environments.

Here are a few examples of floral scents:

- Lavender
- Rose
- Jasmine
- Geranium
- Ylang-Ylang
- Lilac
- Chamomile
- Hibiscus
- Neroli
- Calendula
- Hyssop
- Gardenia
- Hydrangea
- Yarrow

All of these, and more, blend well with woody and citrus (fresh) scents.

Woody

Woody scents are the scents that are naturally warmer and earthier than other scents. When you smell them, they have the tendency to teleport you to mountainous woodlands and mossy, smoky environments. These scents are great for providing a sense of grounding and comfort. Woody scents are the go-to during the cold winter months.

Here are a few examples of woody scents:

- Patchouli
- Sandalwood
- Cedar wood
- Black Spruce
- Balsam Fir
- Cypress
- Juniper
- Blue Spruce
- Palo Santo
- Pine
- Oak Moss
- Black Walnut
- Willow Bark
- Birch Bark

These scents go great with citrus (fresh) as well as floral scents.

Fresh

Anything that reminds you of a bright or invigorating scent is a fresh scent. They are known for being light-hearted and adding a certain level of cleanliness to the area. Not only do they have the power to uplift and reenergize an atmosphere, but they also help to remove bad odors from the room or space.

Here are a few examples of fresh scents:
- Eucalyptus
- Sage
- Lemongrass
- Grapefruit
- Bergamot
- Citronella
- Tangerine
- Verbena
- Basil
- Rosemary
- Thyme
- Angelica

These scents work well with peppermint, as well as floral scents like lavender. They also go great with sugary scents and warm scents.

Exotic

Exotic scents are similar to woody scents in that they provide a sense of warmth and comfort. However, these scents aren't necessarily earthy or derived from wooded areas. These scents are more indulgent. Think of them as the desserts of candle fragrances. Anything rich and luxurious can be found in this category.

Here are a few examples of exotic scents:

- Vanilla
- Carmel
- Cinnamon
- Nutmeg
- Chai
- Myrrh
- Fennel
- Coffee
- Frankincense
- Honey
- Caraway
- Clove
- Tarragon
- Cardamom
- Rosewood
- Ginger
- Benzoin
- Saffron

These scents are best paired with citrus (fresh) and woody scents.

The world of scents and fragrances is vast but is arguably the most fun part of candle making. This is where you truly get to show your creativity in a way that isn't visual. If you play around with candle fragrances enough, you will likely come across a combination that others haven't found. Granted, there are some scents that are classic combinations and will always be best sellers.

For example:
- Eucalyptus and mint
- Ginger, grapefruit, and patchouli
- Pomegranate, peony, and honeysuckle
- Coffee and vanilla
- Rose and ginger
- Sage and orange

However, you could create your own scents that can't readily be found in a nearby grocery or convenience store.

Fragrances aren't the only things that make candles great, though. There are other additives people enjoy putting into their candles. As mentioned above, some people will decorate the top of their candles with crystals and small stones. One of the best things about candles is how incredibly versatile they are. You can add nearly anything to your candles to make them unique. Maybe you add a stick of cinnamon to your cinnamon candles or other dried herbs mixed in with the wax.

You can even add glitter to the wax for candles with special effects. That said, by far, the most common candle additive is a dye. Aside from, maybe:
- Parol Oil
- Stearic Powder
- Vybar 103, 260, or 343

Candle Dyes

Before the world of dyes, candles were the color of their wax, and that was the end of it. Then people started to naturally dye their candles with things like turmeric and beet juice. Natural dyes are still viable options today and are the eco-friendly option for candle dyes, but there are other options as well.

Some people resort to food coloring for deep colors, but there are also wax dye pellets that you can insert into the wax while you warm it up. Stirring the dye, you can see the gradual change of color. The candle's size and how deep of a color you are looking for will determine how many pellets to add. A good rule of thumb is to always start with one and add more if necessary.

You might even come up with a way to make swirls in the colors of your candle. When the candle is burned, the swirls might disappear, but this is a great selling point because it shows how much work you put into creating the candle.

Luster Spray

Traditionally, an additive can be incorporated as you are mixing the wax. Luster spray is still added to the candle, but not until the very end. The purpose of the spray is to leave the candle with a glossy finish. This gives it the effect that it is always melting or wet.

Luster spray is a niche-specific additive. You might not end up using it in your products, but it's always fun to get creative with it!

But enough about your craft—let's get down to business!

Chapter 4: Making Physical Changes to Support Your Dream

You can mess around with different candle styles and fragrances all day long, but if you don't have a space you can feel productive in, then your business won't ever get off the ground. The thing about doing what you love for a living is that sometimes it can be hard to see it and respect it as a job. When it doesn't feel like work, it's hard to call it work. This has many advantages like self-growth and fulfilling your dreams. However, there are a few disadvantages as well, and finding the motivation to fill order can—ironically—be one of them.

This is typically what happens when people try to turn their hobby into a business:

The person is really excited at first and has a ton of creative energy and ideas for the business. The planning and networking begin. The person creates their site or shop and sells a few items. They are on cloud nine and couldn't possibly imagine doing anything else.

* Cue the winds of change *

You start to get several orders a week and realize just how much work it is for you to create even one candle. There's a chance you become overwhelmed and begin losing the motivation to fill a single order.

First, it's crucial to understand just how much work it is to run your own business as it continues to grow. You will constantly be working, especially for the first few years. Ideally, the business would continue to grow and you could one day stop creating the candles yourself. Those are long-term goals, though.

Second, creating a legitimate and productive workspace is the key to success as someone that works from home. It is impossible to get hours' worth of productive work done when your workspace is in an area of the home you despise, or your workspace is too small and unorganized.

Developing a Workspace

You have to love your workspace as much as you love your work. And if you are choosing to start your own business, chances are you love your work quite a bit. Before you make any rash decisions, you must first go over your needs. As a beginning candle-making business, you most likely won't need a building at the start.

Still, I have included information both on home offices and some advice on how to purchase a building for your business.

Tips for Home Workspace Development

Below are four tips that could help you create the business you've always dreamed of simply by creating the perfect home workspace.

1. Workspace Selection

The great thing about working for yourself is the fact that you can adjust your work schedule around the needs of your family or the other areas of your life. However, as a candlemaker, you still need a space that is tailor-made for candle making. It will be the place you return to, day-in and day-out, to fill orders and create new products for your shop. In other words, the layout of the space has to promote such productivity. It's no longer enough to decorate an area for increased productivity. It's now known that it all boils down to the layout of the room or space.

For candle making, it is always best to work in an area that is generally open and has a few windows. Of course, the layout isn't the only deciding factor for a professional home workspace, but candle making in a cramped space isn't necessarily ideal. Candlemakers need elbow room and a space that is well-ventilated to avoid fragrance headaches.

2. Plan the Space

It can be exciting to create a workspace for your business, but that doesn't mean you have to go out and buy everything all at once. First, you should probably plan the area out. At least get a general idea or concept for the space. That will help you answer some of the productive questions before you even get to the store.

Here are a few things you might consider having in your workspace, aside from the necessary equipment and tools:

- Furniture
- Artwork
- A plant or two
- Some fun knick-knacks

Planning all of these things will help you envision the perfect set-up to maximize productivity. One of the most important things to consider is if you have room for movement. As a candlemaker, you won't need a huge space to get the job done, but it would definitely be nice to have a little walking room.

You must also consider the fact that you'll need access to a stove or burner. The garage can be a nice place for work, but if there's no electricity in your garage, it'll be impossible for you to have a workspace in there.

3. Safety First

When making candles, the biggest safety concern is the risk of fire or broken glass. If you are going to launch a business, you will need to make sure there is enough space to include any and all safety precautions mandated by law. That said, you will also need to make sure you aren't violating any zoning laws. Typically, candle-making businesses don't require heavy machinery, so zoning laws shouldn't be anything to worry about.

Still, there is an entire chapter later on that covers all the laws and ways to protect yourself as a business owner. Planning these things out is crucial before buying any equipment because it could result in the need to return some items or exchange them for something slightly different.

4. Creating the Space

Once you've planned everything out and decided where you will place your workspace, it is time to create it. This means buying all the furniture, equipment, tools, and supplies. Painting the walls if you so desire, buying the safety equipment, and even creating a snack area comes next.

It is your dream workspace. Don't be afraid to personalize it. Remember, the key is for you to want to come to work every day. This also means keeping up with cleaning and maintenance. One of the biggest enemies of a candle is dust. Be sure to keep your area clean. It not only shows you the respect you deserve but ensures your candles are always high-quality and clean.

Put it this way:

If you don't have enough respect for your business to create and maintain a meaningful workspace, then this probably isn't the right avenue for you. If candle making is your mission, you will command respect and confidence in a way that you might not be able to in other areas of life.

Of course, commanding that respect might mean you have to buy yourself the space you deserve. Whether it's a small building or a walk-in closet-sized studio, as long as you can comfortably get your work done, that is what matters.

Tips for Buying a Building

Buying a shop might not be feasible before you've made your first sale, but the following are great tips to have when the time comes to buy your first building.

Financial Evaluation

Before you even begin looking for a place, you must evaluate your finances. It is recommended to hire a financial expert to help you go through everything with a fine-toothed comb. Buying a commercial property is nothing to take lightly. Not only do your finances need to be evaluated before purchase, but the property's value does as well. The last thing anyone wants is for their building to suffer because of where they are located.

Some might say that location isn't everything, especially in candle making. If you don't have your doors open for walk-in orders and just use the shop as a place to create the candles, there is no need for a marketable property. However, if your long-term goal is to one day open your doors to the public, you will be glad you evaluated the property's market value before purchase.

It's always better to be safe than sorry, especially when dealing with real estate.

LLC and the 504 Loan

This may be redundant, but your business will need to be registered as a Limited Liability Company (LLC) or another similar business entity. Once you are legally recognized as a business, you can become eligible for the Small Business

Administration 504 Loan. This loan specifically helps small businesses buy real estate and equipment at a lower rate.

This loan is amazing for small businesses because it allows you the opportunity to buy a commercial property with as low as 10% down at a lower fixed rate.

Buying a building or shop might not be the first thing on your list when starting a candle-making business, but depending on your long-term goals for the business, the above-stated information quickly becomes invaluable. Thinking about the long-term might also help you create a real workspace for your business as it stands today. It can give you something to look forward to and to work toward obtaining.

Creating a Schedule

Once you have created a proper and productive workspace, you will want to come up with a schedule for yourself. The great thing about working for yourself is the freedom to work when you want. However, so many people make the mistake of not creating a solid schedule for themselves. What tends to happen is the work takes a back seat. It continuously gets pushed off as something that can be done later, and then 'later' never comes.

Although working for yourself means you can technically work whenever, it doesn't mean you should necessarily approach it this way. The business itself requires a certain level of respect, and time management is a large part of that respect. You must find the hours of the day that you seem to be the most productive and stick to those times.

The worst part about starting your own business is the fact that you will most likely have a day job until your dream job (your business) gets off the ground. That means that the only free time you get, you spend working on your dreams. This schedule will seem hectic and very tiresome for a while. It will feel like you are constantly working, and it might even feel like you are working hard for nothing at times.

Below we cover tips to not only help you manage your time wisely, but information on how to stay motivated during the rough days of working two jobs.

Tips for Mastering Time Management

Mastering the art of time management is the best thing you can do for yourself and your growing business. The trick to mastering time management is to first understand that it takes constant re-evaluation. Anytime you take on a new workload or something in your life changes, it is recommended to evaluate the way you currently manage your time and adjust it accordingly. Things are always changing, so you can't expect your work schedule to stay the same either.

Setting Goals

Proper goal setting is the foundation of time management. It seems to be easier for people to set long-term goals, but unfortunately, that isn't what we are talking about. In terms of time management, short-term goals are far more important. Other than the length of time it takes to achieve each goal, the main difference between long-term and short-term goals is how specific they are. Typically, short-term goals require much more detail if they are expected to be realized in the allotted time.

The great thing about short-term goals is you can make as many as you want. When it comes to your business and managing your time, daily and weekly goals will help you stay on track. Set goals that are specific to each day. Every night before you go to bed, create a list of goals for the next day. Some might call this a "to-do list," but for productivity purposes, we will call this your daily goals. These are easily obtainable goals that can even include things like relaxation, for instance, because everyone needs a reminder to take a step back and relax every now and then.

Your weekly goals could be related to your workload or simply the way you want to feel or think about your work by the end of the week. If your goal is to feel accomplished, what will it take to create that feeling within yourself? Your daily goals should reflect this.

Holding yourself accountable in this way helps you prioritize your time and accomplish more of what you desire each day.

Create Time Windows

Prioritizing time is almost always what people mean when they say they want to be better at time management. The unfortunate thing about prioritizing time is that it's a very personal thing. There are a lot of parts at play that the world doesn't see, like your mental health and unforeseen obstacles that pop up seemingly out of nowhere. Fortunately, these things can be used to strengthen your skills. It is all about the way you look at them.

Life moves in a constant flow state, whether we are aware of it or not. Those obstacles that seemingly come up out of thin air aren't random. For every cause, there is an effect, and for every action, there is an equal and opposite reaction. The choices you make and the choices you don't, all define your life, whether you want them to or not.

When you hold yourself accountable for your own life (in every aspect), you naturally become better at prioritizing your time.

That said, here is a little hack to help you get started:

Set time blocks for yourself to get work done! During these time blocks, turn off or silence all distractions. If you must use the Internet, do not allow yourself to get distracted. Use the Internet for work and work only. Set an alarm to go off when your time is up. This will keep you from looking at the clock every five minutes to see how much time has passed. The time of day that you do these time blocks might change, but the length of time you set for yourself should always be the same.

This will give you the feeling of leniency and flexibility within your work schedule, which keeps you from losing steam. Please note that a time block should never exceed more than four hours without a break. You cannot expect yourself to stay focused longer than that and still get something productive done.

Your brain needs the break, which means your business needs the break—**read that again.**

Organization

Organization is extremely important when you run your own business. It helps you maintain a clear insight into your workload as well as the timeline you want to complete your goals. Many people don't fancy the idea of organization and structure, but when you are first starting out, these two things can save your business.

Start by organizing your workspace and strive to clean it every time you use it. Place all of your supplies into specific areas and put everything back where it belongs. Doing this will help you organize your time as well, believe it or not. It will put you in the organizational mindset, and you might even start organizing other areas without even realizing it.

For instance:

Setting specific time blocks each day and setting daily and weekly goals are your first steps toward organizing your time. Take it one step further and do this with the rest of your days and weeks.

I realize that not everyone works better with this type of structure, but in the beginning, it can really help you get a handle on how much time you actually have each day to work. Once you get into a nice workflow, you can become a bit more lenient in this area.

Accountability & Self Discipline

Running your own business is tough, and one of the hardest parts is the fact that you don't have anyone over your shoulder making sure you get everything done on time. You are your own boss. But that's the thing - you have to be your own boss. You must have a sense of self-discipline and accountability, or you will continue to put your work on the back burner.

Starting your own business while still working a day job means you will have to sacrifice most of your free time. Remember your long-term goal. Remember why you started. Write it down and place it somewhere you will see often and read it over and over. A year from now, those missed hang-outs and parties won't mean anything in comparison to your dreams coming true. Each year you are willing to sacrifice your free time to accomplish your dreams is a year that sets you up for success.

A lack of accountability and self-discipline are the two greatest things that always get people into trouble when they want to start a business. Don't let it happen to you!

Working Your Day Job to Support Your Dreams

Being a small business owner comes with its many challenges, but we will talk about that more in Chapter 11. One of the main complaints people have when they decide to start a business has to do with their day job. They either don't want to continue working it but have to in order to fund their dreams of launching their business; or, they complain, feeling like they are constantly working and never have time for themselves. It's true. Starting your own business isn't for the faint of heart. It usually takes someone that loves to work, and even then, there are days when you will just want to quit.

That said, just because you own a small business doesn't mean you will be working 80 hours a week for the rest of your life. Although, New York Enterprise Report conducted a study in which they found that 33% of small business owners say they work more than 50 hours a week. However, spending 50 hours a week doing what you love feels like working part-time anywhere else. If you think about it, most of the time, you'll be doing things you find fun, things you are passionate about. The "part-time" hours are those spent crunching numbers and scaling your business for growth.

Until the time comes for you to work your dream job full-time, here are a few tips to keep you going:

Know Yourself

Knowing oneself is absolutely one of the biggest secrets all successful business owners have in common. If you don't have your mind right, there is no way you'll be able to turn your passions into a business and still be happy when it's all said and done. Knowing oneself is multi-faceted because we are all so complex and unique. Self-discovery is the best gift anyone can give themselves in this life.

When it comes to your business, knowing when to take a break and how to take care of yourself is vital.

There's this saying, and it goes something like:

We are all givers. In one area or another, we give ourselves away. And we all have a Giving Cup. Imagine this Giving Cup is full of water. If you give all of yourself to your work and you never receive or expect to receive anything in return, soon your cup will be empty. Rather, allow yourself the time to give to yourself—practice self-care and filling that cup up until it is over-flowing.

If you always make sure your Giving Cup is over-flowing, it will inevitably spill onto those around you.

In terms of work, remember to take care of yourself and fill your cup up. Then, you can take that over-flowing cup of happiness, determination, and focus and channel it accordingly. This is the best way to get the most productive work done. It will also help you to keep things in perspective while working a day job you don't particularly like. On the days that you feel like giving up or like you can't get any productive work done, take that as a sign that it is time for a mental break. Put your passions down for a night or two and focus on yourself. You'll be surprised what it does for your business.

Know Your Business

The good thing about keeping your day job while you work toward achieving your dreams is that it buys you some time to really get to know your business. Don't be afraid to change your mind either. A lot of people pivot their business before they ever launch. Sure, a candle-making business is pretty self-explanatory on the surface. As you are well aware though, there are many avenues one can take when making candles.

Not only that, but there is branding and marketing to think about as well.

You have a day job that still pays the bills. Use this time wisely to prepare all areas of your business as much as you can. There will inevitably be changes that take place once the launch occurs and most likely multiple other times throughout the life of the business. In a nutshell, that's just how business works. You have to be willing to constantly evolve with your business.

Know the Industry

Having a day job also gives you the time to learn all there is to know about the candle-making industry. Rather than coming home from work and watching TV until you go to bed, create the habit of reading about the industry! Trust me, it might feel like work at first, but you'll soon realize that reading and learning about things you love is just as entertaining as your favorite TV show. The only difference is the reading gets you one step closer to working full-time at your dreams!

Don't Get Ahead of Yourself

When working toward your dreams, it is easy to think too far into the future and get ahead of yourself. That is your worst enemy, especially when you are still working a day job as well. Remember to take it one step at a time and to cherish each moment for what it is. Doing so will help you learn and appreciate your day job while you have it. Who knows, you might even start to like it!

Chapter 5: Coming Up with a Plan

If you are ever going to launch your dream business and quit your day job for good, you must first create a business plan. This term feels a bit scary at first and can often leave people confused about where to start. The term comes with certain connotations, one of which being that it has to be some lengthy process with business lingo and whatever else.

The fact of the matter is, it's your business. At the end of the day, as long as you can comprehend the business plan, that is what matters most. And yes, there are some business owners that like to create five-year business plans that are usually pretty lengthy. However, when you just want to launch your business and get off the ground, all it takes is a solid 12-month plan to start. Then, around six months in, reevaluate said business plan and go from there. This first business plan isn't as intense as the reputation makes it seem.

When you're eventually ready to create another business plan, you'll already have a nice handle on what to include. Creating this first business plan is the most fun, too, because it's the plan where you get to create your branding style and decide what niche avenue you want to head down.

Below, you will learn all about what to include in your initial business plan. This will hopefully take some of the stress off of the situation. Remember, you can always add to it and revise it later on!

How to Create a Professional Business Plan

Have fun while creating your first business plan with these easy steps:

Creating a Solid Mission Statement

A mission statement is usually one—maybe two—sentences long and has the purpose of explaining the entirety of your business. This alone is enough to give you anxiety.

How am I supposed to properly encompass my entire business in a mere sentence?

For starters, try answering this series of tough questions:

- Identify your target audience:
    - What's their age range?
    - How do they think and feel?
    - What do they do for a living?
    - What are their ideals?
- How will you interact with your customers?
    - Are there customers that might not like your business based on their ideals?
    - Do you plan to send follow-up emails?
    - Will you have an email list and send out promotional emails?
    - Will you mostly have a face-to-face presence or web presence?
- What makes your business unique?
    - What is it that your business offers, aside from candles?

- o Do you donate to charity, give out gifts, or offer a community setting?
- Why should people choose you?

All of these questions are so important, and once you can answer them, they will help you create your mission statement. At its core, it should describe your values while simultaneously answering all the above questions wrapped into three short questions:

- What are you selling?
- How do you plan to sell it?
- Why are you here?
  - o What value do you offer your customers other than your main products?

Let's take Apple, for instance. Apple, as we all know, is an extremely successful business and doesn't show signs of slowing down any time soon.

Here is their mission statement:

"Everything we do, we believe in challenging the status quo. We believe in thinking differently. The way we challenge the status quo is by making products that are beautifully designed and user-friendly; we just happen to make computers. Want to buy one?"

Now, this mission statement is a little longer than suggested, but it gets the job done.

Their "what" factor is, "we just happen to make computers."

Their "how" factor is "making products that are beautifully designed and user-friendly."

Their "why" factor is "challenging the status quo and thinking differently."

Then, they even include a call to action at the very end: "want to buy one?" This little addition is a genius way to make the mission statement more engaging and well-rounded. The only thing that might be worth changing is how they restate themselves by saying, "the way we challenge the status quo is by…" This part doesn't seem to add value to the mission statement. Instead, it adds unnecessary length.

Also, just because this is the first step to creating a business plan doesn't mean it has to be the first thing you do before moving on. In fact, it might be better to save this step for last. Sometimes, we might think we have a nice mission statement until we finish the rest of the business plan and really map out where we want the business to go. So, if you decide to create your mission statement before any other part of the business plan, be sure to revisit it at the end to make sure it still encompasses your business the way you hoped.

Identify and Define Your Target Market/Audience

This is mentioned in the above section as one of the hard questions to answer before beginning. However, it is also something that deserves its own section because defining your audience and target market is hard, and creating products to reflect that decision can be even harder.

Your Target Audience

A target audience is a little different than the target market. The target audience is usually determined by a few different things, while the target market usually refers to the financial aspect and what people can afford as well as the quality of the product. That said, your target market might determine your target audience and vice versa. For instance, if you are looking to appeal to the high-end market, you will typically appeal to the middle-aged target audience as well as some of the younger target audience that grew up with money. Contrarily, those appealing to the mass-market target market will appeal to a wider range of audiences.

There are four main segments to determining your target audience. These four segments are:

- **Demographic:**
  - Age, gender, marital status, education, etc.
- **Psychographic:**
  - Values, interests, beliefs, personality, lifestyle, etc.
- **Behavioral:**
  - Spending habits, brand interactions, and user status
- **Geographical:**
  - Region, city/country, neighborhood, etc.

Depending on your target market, your target audience might be extremely vast. This is good and bad. It can be harder to create campaigns and ads if you have a wide target audience. In this case, it might be better to focus your ads around the special things your candles bring to the table that other candles do not.

Your Target Market

In today's world, it is easy to feel like there isn't enough space in the candle-making industry for another small business. However, with the right branding and target market, there is absolutely room for more! There are three target markets to consider for your business. They are mapped out below. Read through them and decide which of the three your business will thrive in the most.

• Mid-Market:

This is the market that most candlemakers today fall under. These candles have a broad appeal, meaning they have a wide target audience range. You can usually find these candles in common stores like Target or Macy's. Still, these candles are unique in their own way. They have special scents unique to the company and packaging as well. The price range of these candles is usually between 10 and 15 dollars.

• Mass-Market:

Mass-market candles are usually the cheapest market of candles. Small businesses typically aren't in this market because homemade candles are usually too unique and require a higher price. Mass-market candles are usually produced by larger companies and have very basic scents and packaging. You can find these candles at dollar stores and other large retailers. These candles are typically priced between 2 and 10 dollars.

• High-End Market:

High-end market candles are luxury items. You will find these candles in luxury stores like Nordstrom and Saks Fifth Avenue. They also are made with premium wax, fragrances, and packaging. These candles usually have additives in them as well that help them burn longer than other candles. You will typically see these candles priced between 15 and 25 dollars. Some homemade candlemakers will make their candles for this market as well.

It is also important to take the industry and other companies into consideration. Look at your competition. If you are making one-of-a-kind homemade candles, you might not be in competition with large mass-market corporations. Stay focused on your lane of the market, and it will help you identify how to better communicate with your target audience.

Target marketing and knowing your target audience is extremely important in your overall survival as a business in this industry. As briefly mentioned before, candles aren't hard to find nowadays, but that doesn't necessarily mean there isn't a place for you in the industry. Knowing how to communicate with your target audience and understanding which target market you reside in are the two greatest things to help you build a meaningful connection with your customers. As the world progresses, customers are more willing to buy from a small business they feel they can trust than a large corporation. In other words, convenience is no longer everything.

Discover Your Niche

In the candle-making world, finding a niche is as easy as you make it. There aren't too many niches in this industry, which can make the decision a little easier for some. Try not to over-complicate things. Find what works for you and watch your business naturally fall into place.

Here are a few examples of niches we've seen in the past:

- Unique packaging
- Brand-specific scent combinations
- Unique candle names
- Color variations
- Carved candles
- Glitter, stones, or other visual additives
- Long-lasting candles
- A certain percent of each candle going toward a charitable cause

The great thing about these niches is that you can eventually create products that align with each niche, which means you have a chance to test them all out. At first, it is best to stick with one. Work to develop one line of candles specific to a given niche. Then, when you see success with this line of candles, you can begin exploring other niches.

Another great thing about the different candle niches is that it allows so much room for creativity. Yes, there are many candle companies in the world, but you can still find an avenue that many of the other candle companies haven't ventured down before. You can still pave your own way, in other words.

For example:

Finding pillar candles with pictures painted around the outside is rare. You'd have to do some research on the different paint that would be safe to use and still work well on the candle, but this is an extremely creative avenue that not many people take. Most of the large corporations just use glass jars and try to stand out with specific scent variations or wick types.

As a small business, you might have to get a little more creative to stand out, but that doesn't mean it's impossible by any means.

Create Your Branding Identity

Many business owners find that creating their brand name and identity are the easiest parts of their business plan. Oftentimes, before people do any industry research or even begin their business plan, they have an idea of what they want their brand name to be. For others, making the actual decision of what to call their business can become difficult because—all of a sudden—they feel all this pressure to pick the perfect name.

Rarely do you hear of a business changing its name. This is because once you've established yourself in a given industry and market, your customers know you by a certain name. Changing your name is something you want to try to avoid because you would then have to re-establish yourself. Larger corporations can get away with things like this more often than small businesses. So, how do you pick the best name for your business?

Deciding on a Name

Typically, when deciding on a name, it is best to go with something catchy and unique but also something that is easy to remember.

Here are some things to think about:

- Remember your niche.
- Think about what makes your business unique.
- What part of the business are you most passionate about?
- Remember your target audience and what resonates with them.

At the end of the day, picking a name that your customers love is just as important—if not more important—than picking a name you love. Run your suggested business names by a few trusted peers or your business partner to see what their first impression is.

Once you have landed on a name you believe represents your business well, search for domain names online. In today's world, it is extremely hard to survive without an online presence of some sort, especially as a small business. Having an easy-to-remember domain name is just as important as the business name itself. Ideally, you want your domain name to be the exact same as your business name. Not only that, but you have to make sure that there isn't another candle-making business out there with your name. If there is, you could run into some legality issues later on.

Logo and Color Scheme

Aside from the name, branding is heavily dependent on your chosen logo and general color scheme. This definitely takes more work and thought than the name. Many have done studies on colors in the past and their impact on society. It's been proven that colors carry their own frequency or vibration, and these frequencies can make people feel a certain way. People's past experiences with certain colors can cause them to associate a given color with an old memory.

Not only can your color scheme generate a certain emotional appeal and general schematic expectation, but your logo has the power to imprint itself in the memory of your customers. The color of the logo plays a big role in this, but probably more important than the color is the logo's design.

As a small business owner working a day job, it might be hard to find the extra cash to spend on your dreams. You might find yourself with a tight budget. However, if you are going to spend money on anything before you launch your business, it should be your domain (as stated above) and your logo design. Most people that start their own business aren't graphic design professionals. Spend the extra money to hire a design specialist to bring your vision to life. They will take your creative vision and add their expertise and most likely turn your logo into something better than you ever envisioned.

What Is Your Basic Startup Budget?

On the topic of budgets, be sure to include your ideal startup budget in your business plan. You might be creating this business plan to serve as your plan for the next six to twelve months, but when it comes to your budget, it is best to revisit it monthly or at least bi-monthly.

Here are some things you should include in your budget:

- Supply costs
- Equipment costs
- Workspace costs
- Logo/domain costs

You will also want to draft out a general overhead budget as well. Overhead costs are anything that is ongoing. For instance, you will have to buy more supplies at some point. You might also consider insurance, which we will get into more later. If you pay to have someone create a website for you, this will need to be included in your budget as well.

When you start listing out all of your expenses, it might feel like a lot at first. As a general rule of thumb, most small business owners budget $1,000 to launch their business. Bear in mind, though, that these are initial expenses. It won't always cost you this much because things like your workspace and equipment will only need to be budgeted for once. When you launch and start making money off your products, you will make that budget back relatively quickly. From there, business expenses won't feel as jarring.

Developing Your Product Line (On Paper)

Developing your product line is another fun aspect of creating your initial business plan. You probably have all of these ideas in your head and prototypes of the candles you plan to sell. Now it's time to develop your line on paper. Write down all of the inclusions you want in your first line of candles.

It's important to note that keeping it simple is the way to go, especially for your first few line launches. The smaller the product line, the easier it'll be to manage. This is a great way for you to dip your toes in the water before you really know how to swim. It is also a good idea to run your product line by your business partner and even other businesses you've been networking with. We will talk more about networking with businesses in a minute, but doing so will help you get an idea of how simple to make your first product line.

Even if you plan to create unique and one-of-a-kind candles, research the best-selling candles on the market—whether they are mass-produced or one-of-a-kind like the candles you plan to make. See what works in the industry first. It might be better to save the more unique candles for later launch dates once you've established yourself and drawn in customers. Again, the simpler you make your first launch, the better because you will have many other unforeseen considerations coming your way shortly after your launch.

Where Will You Sell?

This part of the business plan might not seem like a huge decision, but there are quite a few small details that you will have to consider. Chances are, you plan to create your own Shopify website to sell from as well as selling on another site like Etsy or a social media platform. Depending on your following base, it might be best for you to start with your social media platform. However, if you don't already have a following, a Shopify website and advertising on Facebook might be your best bets.

You might also consider setting up local pop-up locations in parking lots or at local fairs and markets, but this is more of a long-term consideration.

At first, you simply need to decide:

- If you want to have an online presence
- If you want to have a local presence
- Where the online and physical locations will be

If you want to create your own website, Shopify is the best for those looking to sell merchandise. It is easy to build a website and get selling quickly. A few other website builders worth noting are Wix, WordPress, and Squarespace. Wix is probably the most beginner-friendly of all the choices because it offers templates that make creating your site even easier. When you use a template, you no longer have to build the website out entirely. You simply can change the design to personalize it to your wants and needs.

Once you have created the website and you feel it is ready to publish, that is where networking and marketing really come into play. We will get into these topics more shortly. You can have the greatest candles ever, but without impeccable marketing and networking, it will be next to impossible for you to get your business off the ground. This is especially true for those that don't have the social media following mentioned above.

Legality Checklist

This topic will also have its own chapter later on, but there are a few legal matters that should be included in your initial business plan. Create a checklist of the legal things necessary to cover before launching your business, as well as the proper people to contact to get the best information.

Below is a helpful checklist to get you started, but keep in mind that everyone is different. There might be more people you need to contact, or you might feel you can wait to contact certain people until after your initial launch. Remember, it is perfectly fine and legal for you to launch your first and even second line of candles before taking any huge legal steps. If you want to make sure that your business will survive before contacting legal professionals, that is understandable and reasonable.

Here is a checklist for your convenience:

- **Insurance Professional:**
    - Of all the legality issues, insurance is something extremely important for every business to have. As a small business, liability insurance might be the most beneficial insurance package for your business. You might not need anything more than that, but

it's always best to consult a professional before taking the plunge.

- **Licenses and Permits:**
  - o Things like zoning permits are usually only necessary if you buy a building for your business or plan to turn your garage into a legal shop. That said, at the beginning of your candle-making career, you most likely won't be filling many orders at once. Therefore, you can safely and legally create your candles in the comfort of your own home if need be. Still, consult a professional to get a complete run-down of this information.
- **Incorporating Your Business:**
  - o For tax purposes, incorporating your business is something that will be necessary the moment you launch. It will also help you when it comes to writing off things for your business, like the equipment, supplies, and things for your workspace. All of those items will be tax write-offs when you incorporate your business.
  - o Some business structures to look at:
    - Limited Liability Company (LLC)
    - Sole proprietorship
    - General partnership
    - S Corporation
    - C Corporation

You will also want to think about contacting an accountant and attorney. These are both unbiased professionals that will give you objective advice on things to consider for your business. All of these professionals have experience with first-time business owners and small businesses, as well as established companies and beyond. Just like anything else, it is important to do your research and consult with a few different professionals. You will come across more advice and greater knowledge by doing this.

Again, this is solely a checklist placed here for your convenience. It is by no means to be accepted as professional legal advice. It is a list of suggestions for you to think about as a future business owner. Please consult with professionals before making any major decisions.

Additional Business Plan Help

You can also check out www.alexandercowan.com/business-model-canvas-templates for a one-page business canvas to help create your very first business plan. It removes the guesswork and allows for more free-flowing ideas to come. This canvas ensures you answer all the tough questions. The greatest thing you can do for yourself is to take the time to research each question and answer them with as much detail as possible. Don't just research the positive things, either - it is just as important to research the struggles that other candle-making business owners have experienced.

It's also important to note that following through with your business plan and sticking to it is essential. It is the detailed business plans that are successful, but ensuring that you constantly revisit the plan to see if you are on the right track is just as important. Those that make their business plan and then stuff it in a folder to never be seen again are those that tend to struggle down the line.

Be proud of your business plan. After all, it is your business, written out in paper form. Post it up on a wall that you look at often to remind yourself of where you see your business going.

Networking

Networking can be talked about in two different ways: you can network business-to-business, and you can network with your customers via marketing tactics. We will talk about the marketing form of networking in a little bit. For now, let's focus on how to build your business via networking with other professionals in the industry as well as business professionals in general.

It Takes a Village

As a one-person small business, you might be at it alone the majority of the time. But, it is always better to have a few key players at your side when need be, even if those players are your spouse or a business partner/assistant. Even if said partner or spouse doesn't do anything for the business itself, the fact that they are there for mental and moral support can make all the difference. Take all the help and support you can get, especially while you are still working a day job. These types of people will help motivate you to continue on and serve as a reminder for why you started in the first place.

Consult with other candle-making business owners. They will provide you with more insight than any amount of research ever could. These types of people have been in the field. They know the drill. They can give you real-life examples of good and bad business tactics. They can show you what works and what doesn't. When consulting with other businesses, don't stop at just one or two. Try to find a wide variety of experiences. Contact those that have been in business for years or decades even, and also try to find companies that are in their first year of business.

Doing so will give you great insight into how to become an established business in this industry. That said, looking at new businesses that are still in their first year will also give you great insight on how to get your business off the ground in this climate of the economy.

At this stage in the game, it is no surprise what 2020 did for the economy—however, some of the greatest businesses launched in an economic downturn. Take Airbnb, for example. There aren't many people that hear this name today and don't have something to say about their experience with the company. This company was founded during the recession in 2008, and it is a travel-based company. During times of recession, the last thing you think people would be doing is spending money on travel, but they did, and they do! Even during the end of 2020, more and more people started traveling again.

It is businesses like these that give the world hope for a better tomorrow. This could be the reason that people buy into them so much, because of the fact that they were founded during a time when most of the country or world felt vulnerable about spending money.

That is why it is so important to talk with beginning and established candle-making businesses. They have the hands-on experience you are looking for. It wouldn't hurt to try to reach out to a few large candle-making corporations, either. Even if you don't plan on entering the mass-market or high-end market, contact businesses from every market to see how their candles and business tactics vary across the board.

You might even find a few companies that are willing to let you sit in on their production and marketing processes. Don't be afraid to ask for what you want. You never know who will say yes.

Chapter 6: Quality Assurance and Safety

If you've made it this far in your candle-making journey, you most likely understand that there is a certain level of precision to creating quality candles that are safe and effective. It is more than just an art form, and if you turn it into a business, then the layers of quality assurance become multi-faceted. You no longer only have to care about the quality of your product, but the quality of your website and business overall.

Safety is also a vital concern in candle making for the simple fact that you are dealing with an open flame willingly being placed inside the homes of your customers. The last thing anyone wants to worry about causing damage to their home is a candle they bought online.

In this chapter, we will dive into what it takes to not only develop quality candles, but to stay on top of quality assurance in general and different safety tips all new candlemakers should be aware of.

Tips for Quality Assurance

Quality assurance and maintenance typically go hand-in-hand. Essentially, the goal is to go over your entire business with a fine-toothed comb. Being the owner of your own business, you can come up with how often you think it is appropriate to run a quality assurance check, but the more often, the better.

Products

You will likely want to make sure you are creating the highest quality candles possible for your projected price range. A large part of ensuring quality is the supplies you use. We mentioned all of these earlier in the book, but the container, wax type, wick type, and fragrance/additives determine your candle quality right from the start. However, there are a few other things that go into ensuring your candles burn as intended.

There is a specific ratio to consider before choosing the wick. Wicks come in different sizes, and the size of the container you decide to use will determine which size wick will work best for that particular candle. Because of the number of variables involved in this ratio, check out this resource at: https://www.candlescience.com/learning/wick-guide. This is meant to help you find a wick that is right for your candle.

Efficiency

This will look different for everyone, but mastering time management is a huge part of being a successful business owner. When you are first starting out, you might be willing to spend a little more time on things to ensure they are done correctly, but once you've mastered your craft, efficiency is the next order of business.

Efficiency is something you will have to keep in mind throughout the entirety of your business. It is a part of quality assurance that you might excel at one month and struggle with the next. This is also an important lesson in patience as well. If you know this month was flooded with new orders you weren't used to receiving, remember to be patient with yourself if you weren't as efficient with your time as you usually are. That said, use it as an opportunity to learn as well. It is a time to see where your efficiency lacked and how you can improve it later to accommodate for the influx in orders.

Customer Service

Sure, your business wouldn't exist without your products, but it also wouldn't exist without satisfied customers either. In the age of technology, customer service can make or break your business. Everyone leaves reviews, and if they aren't avid review writers, then they are most likely the type that only writes a review when the experience was subpar. Too many negative reviews, and you all of a sudden lose all credibility with your target audience.

One great way to perform customer service quality assurance is to consistently read through and address your customer reviews. Something else people love to see is a business that responds to their reviews, whether they are positive or negative. The public wants to see just how submerged you are in your community.

You can also stay on top of customer service simply by running promotions and adding gifts inside of orders as a token of appreciation. Show your customers how much you appreciate them, and they just might help you grow your business by telling their friends about you.

Website

Website quality assurance is extremely important as well, and it will most likely take longer than everything else because there is so much involved in it. Because we live in the age of technology, your website is the face of your business. This is especially true for those who don't plan to have a physical location. That is why it is so crucial for your website to be user-friendly, appealing, and bug-free.

Below is a list of a few other things to check during your website quality assurance checks:

- **Check All Buttons for Efficacy:**
    - o Nothing messes up the user's experience like clicking a button that sends you to the wrong page or doesn't work at all. It is important to check all website buttons consistently. Sometimes a link could break that worked properly a few months ago.
- **Communication:**
    - o You might find it beneficial to have some sort of live chat or forum on your site as a way to better communicate with your customers. This is a great way to build that customer-client relationship, but only if it works properly! Live chats take a fair amount of maintenance as well, so ensure it's effective before launching it on your site because, trust me, your customers will use it as soon as you make it available to them! Customers love to feel like they can

easily contact one of the business professionals, especially the owner.

- **Blog:**
  - o You may decide to add a blog to your site. Blogs are a proven way to help market a business and rank higher on Google. That said, blogs also come with their set of maintenance as well, including crunching the numbers to see if your articles are bringing in viewers like they are meant to. It is also a separate part of your site which means it will need its own performance checks to ensure all the buttons work effectively and everything runs smoothly. You might also have clients comment on the articles, so replying to comments is sometimes necessary.
- **Product Page:**
  - o Above all else, the product page is by far the most important page of your site. This page will need constant performance checks and need to be visually appealing and user-friendly.

There's a lot that goes into creating and maintaining a website. Whether you research and learn how to properly maintain on your own or hire help, the most important thing is that it gets done and gets done properly. You may find it worth it down the line to hire help to complete consistent quality assurance checks. However, most business owners do this themselves at first as a way to save money.

Safety Tips

Candle making has turned into something that is marketed as an easy hobby for anyone to try. This is true in a sense. However, there are some inherent dangers to candle making. The more candles you make at once, the higher the risk.

Below is a list of safety tips to keep your workspace safe as well as your customers:

- **Equipment:**
    - When you first get into candle making, it is easy to let the creativity run wild and begin making candles in all kinds of different containers. However, some containers aren't fit for candles because they could crack or explode from the heat. It is crucial to know if the glass is safe for candle making before you experiment with it.
    - Temperature is also the name of the game when making the candle, so it's important to always have a properly working thermometer with you. If you pour the wax into the glass before it cools all the way, the glass will break.
- **Materials:**
    - Always use wax that is made for candles. Otherwise, it can lead to upper respiratory problems when the customer burns the candle in their home. It is also a potential fire hazard to use wax that isn't graded for candles.
    - Wicks are also important to pay attention to. If the wick is too large for the candle, it will create

soot when burned, which also leads to respiratory problems. Not only that, but a wick that is too large for the candle will make the candle hotter than it needs to be and can cause it to explode.

o Fragrance oils are great for candles but not necessarily for your skin. Unlike essential oils, fragrance oils are too strong for the skin. If you get any of the oils in your pores, it could irritate your skin or even make you sick. Always wear gloves when adding the oil, and be sure to wash your hands immediately if any gets on your fingers.

- **Workspace:**
    o It is important for customers to place their candles in well-ventilated areas away from furniture and fabrics, but it's equally as important to make the candles in a well-ventilated area. Again, the fumes from the fragrance oils can lead to respiratory issues after prolonged periods of time.

    o Always have an area specifically for allowing the candles to cool. It's important to keep a clean and organized workspace, so you don't have to worry about anything falling onto your products and ruining them before they get a fair chance to cool and harden.

    o Of course, be sure to wear protective gear, like close-toed shoes, while working with hot wax and glass. You never know when an accident will occur, so it's always better to be prepared.

These safety tips aren't meant to scare you away from pursuing your dream. Rather, they are a reminder that while candle making is fun and allows for immense creativity, there are some precautions that should always be considered.

Chapter 7: Pricing

There are many factors to consider before coming up with a price for your candles. For starters, will you be selling to wholesalers? Will you sell online in the global market or just in your local market? Typically, most small business owners start by selling online as well as at their local market if they get the chance. Selling online is by far the quickest way to reach a broader audience in today's world. You don't necessarily need a large wholesaler anymore to get the job done.

That said, if you reach out to wholesalers and eventually expand your market by selling to them as well as selling for yourself, this will only increase your profits later on because the wholesaler might reach an audience you haven't yet. The wholesaler has their own set customer base, and when your candles sit on their shelves, it will be hard not to sell. That is one of the major perks of selling to wholesalers, even if you don't make as much money off each candle.

Below is a breakdown of how much a candle typically costs to make and how to ensure that cost stays as low as possible to increase your profit margin. We will also cover how to price your candles for wholesalers compared to retail.

How to Break Down the Cost of Your Candles

As a business owner, you will have many goals for your business, but one of the top goals is to make a profit. After all, there is no business without a profit margin. There are a few different tricks to help you gain a bigger profit margin, but the main thing is buying your supplies in bulk. When you buy things in bulk, you can get them at a lower price, which inevitably lowers the cost it takes to make each of your candles. The lower the cost to make the candle, the higher the profit margin.

Here's a quick rundown of what typically goes into making each candle:

• Candle container
• Wax
• Wick
• Fragrance
• Additives
• Dyes
• Labels and packaging

Say you want every candle to have a unique container. Maybe you try to find vintage glass jars and other things graded for candle making to help your candles stand out against the competition. If that is the case, you might not be able to save a lot of money in this category, but every other supply you can easily find in bulk. You can find candle containers in bulk as well if you aren't worried about their uniqueness. Just remember that while unique candles do stand out against the crowd, they can be harder to price reasonably because they cost so much to make.

On the topic of bulk purchasing, it is also better to buy all of your bulk supplies from the same provider. When you do this, you only have to worry about one shipping cost, which will also lower your overall costs. The more providers you buy from, the more you pay in shipping. You also want to look for a supply provider that is closer to you, if possible. If you try to ship something across the country, your shipping costs will jump considerably.

Still, there might be one company in particular that has amazing fragrances that you are dying to use in your candles. It might cost more, but if it means you get to create the candles you desire and your candles are higher quality because of it, then it might be worth it to you to pay a little extra for those supplies.

Typically, from bulk supply sites, they will also offer flat rate shipping costs. This is something you absolutely want to watch for and is the main reason why you should buy in bulk. The fragrance oils tend to be the most expensive part of the candle for most people unless you are looking to buy expensive containers. That said, with flat rate shipping, if you buy one bottle of fragrance at the flat rate shipping cost of, let's say, $8.00, you could potentially buy twenty bottles at the same shipping cost with flat rate shipping. As you can see, it is far more worth it to buy everything at once, especially when it comes to your fragrances.

However, when you are looking to create your first candle line and you still aren't sure which fragrances you want to use, this will take more experimenting. In turn, the more you experiment, the more you spend trying to create this prototype. When you finally settle on a combination you like, go ahead and buy more than you think you need of every supply. You will use it! That is the one great thing about candle-making supplies—the wax never really goes bad. The fragrance oil typically has a shelf-life of about one year, though, so keep that in mind as well.

Here's How to Break Down the Cost of Each Candle

To continue with shipping costs, if you purchase containers, lids for those containers, wax, wicks, and fragrances (additives and dyes), the shipping will usually run you about $20.00 per supply. So, when you break down the price of each supply, you will want to include this $20.00 each time.

Wax

Let's start with the wax. You first want to break down the cost per ounce. You can buy a large (60lb) bag of wax for about $100.00. So, add $100.00 + $20.00 = $120.00.

Then, you want to take that $120.00 and divide it by 60lbs (the total weight of the wax), which equals about $2.00 per pound. You can break that down even further, which leaves you with about $0.15 per ounce.

For an 8oz candle, that comes to about $.70 per candle just in the wax, including shipping.

Wicks

You can buy a bulk bag of 200 wicks for around $17.00 after tax.

$17.00 + $20.00 (shipping) = $37.00

Then you divide $37.00 / 200 wicks (total wicks in the bag), and that equals about $.19 per wick.

Containers

You can find a pack of 120 containers for about $25.00. Add that to your $20.00 shipping costs to get $45.00.

Then take $45.00 and divide that by the total 120 containers, and you will get about $.38 per container.

Lids

There are bulk boxes of 144 lids for about $28.00 after tax. Add that to your $20.00 shipping to get $48.00.

Take the $48.00 and divide it by the total number of lids which is 144, and you will get $.35 per lid.

Fragrance

This is where things get a little more expensive. You can buy 64 ounces of fragrance oil for about $90.00. So, add that to your $20.00 shipping costs to get $110.00.

Then, take the $110.00 and divide it by the total 64 ounces to get about $1.40 per ounce of fragrance oil.

Now, to break this down to cost per pound of wax, typically, people use about 10 percent fragrance oil for every pound of wax. This equals out to about 1.6, which is about $2.20 per pound of wax. You can make three 8-ounce candles per one pound of wax, so you take $2.20 and divide that by 3 to get your total, which is $.75 cost of fragrance per candle.

You will repeat this process for any other additives and labels you purchase as well.

Now, the final step is to add that all together.

$.70 (wax) + $.19 (wick) + $.38 (container) + $.35 (lid) + $.75 (fragrance) = $2.37

So, $2.37 is the cost it takes for you to make one 8-ounce candle in this example. The cost it takes for you to make your candle might vary, but this is the general formula you will follow.

Wholesale Pricing vs. Retail Pricing

Determining the price of wholesale and retail is where you start to see your profit margin come alive. A good rule of thumb to follow is to double the price of the cost per candle for wholesale and then to double that price for retail.

Given the above example of $2.37 per candle, multiply that by two to get $4.74. You would sell to wholesalers for $4.74 per candle.

Then to sell the candle on your website, multiply $4.74 by two to get $9.48. The same candle would then be sold for $9.48 on your website.

As your company grows, you can raise this price to the next standard, which is to triple your price for wholesalers and then to double that price for retail.

$2.37 * 3 = $7.11 (wholesale price)

$7.11 * 2 = $14.22 (retail price)

Again, your prices might be higher or lower depending on what you add to your candles. Typically, the label and packaging will raise this price a bit, but these price points are generally what candles go for in the mass-market. Of course, larger candles will cost more and smaller candles, less.

Again, if you feel your craft deserves a higher price for the same cost to create, that is up to you as well. At the end of the day, it is your business, and if you feel you put more artistic expression into your candles that deserves to be compensated, that is your call.

Chapter 8: Labeling and Packaging

Labeling and packaging also provide a functional purpose. After all, both are needed to tell the customer what they are buying as well as to sending the customer their product. The story doesn't end there, though. Your labels and packaging are an extra space to share your story and make a lasting impression on your customers. Your labels could be the difference between customers buying your candles at a retailer or purchasing another company's candles instead.

Yes, labeling and packaging both come with added costs, especially if you customize your packaging. That tends to be more expensive than creating customized labels. However, it pays off in the end to have unique packaging. It might be something the customer throws out, but it shows how much you really do care about your business. Not only that, but the customer could potentially reuse the packaging to send out another piece of mail. This is essentially free advertising for you.

You, of course, will have to choose packaging that can accommodate the size of your candles and any other fun gifts you decide to include with each purchase. Fragility must also be taken into account. Candles are fragile and require some sort of support during shipment. There are different ways to customize this as well, or you can add your own little flair and create your own support for the candle.

Packaging can get expensive and is something you will want to include in the pricing of your candles. This is especially true for those going with customized packaging. Labeling is a little more affordable, but you still might consider purchasing your own labeler. You will want one that allows for customized designs to be added to it, and it will be well worth the investment later on. Perhaps at first, you could have someone else make the labels for you. Then, when you sell a few candles, invest that profit into a labeler for your business. You definitely won't regret it.

How Are You Selling Your Candles?

We have mostly talked about packaging in terms of online buyers that will need their candle shipped. However, you might also sell your candles at markets and other pop-up areas. In this case, the buyer might not need an entire box. Rather, a cute bag to put the candle in and some nice wrapping paper to ensure it doesn't break on their walk to their car would do nicely. If you sell your candles at a retailer, there is little to no need for packaging.

Chances are, though, that most of your beginner sales will all be made online. Therefore, the shipping-style packaging mentioned above will most likely be your go-to packaging for a while.

Tell a Story

Tailor your labeling and packaging toward your target audience. You should always have your target audience at the forefront of your mind with every business decision. Ask yourself what they would want to see on your labels and what type of packaging they would appreciate. Maybe you are going the eco-friendly route and would prefer to choose biodegradable packaging or packaging made from recycled materials.

The design should also tell a story, though. This is where your logo comes into play. It was mentioned earlier, but investing in a professional logo should be one of the first things you spend money on. You may have to pick and choose what to invest in at the very beginning, but a logo should definitely be one of them. Once you have the logo, it is yours forever and can easily be placed on a label or box.

Your logo may end up being a very minute part of each label, but it is crucial to have it on there so people know who they're buying from. This is not only a way for them to find your company again later, but a way for you to get your name out there as well. Say a customer buys your candle and places it in their home - every person that comes into their home might smell the candle and want to know where it's from. They can easily look at the label and know where to go the next time they need a candle.

That said, make sure your logo is sent to you in a vector file format. That is the only way you'll be able to add it to a label.

Design Content

As mentioned, the design of your label is extremely important. It is typically the first and last impression the customer has of your business. Yes, they might order the candle from your Etsy or Shopify site, but when they think of your candles, they won't be thinking of those things. They will be thinking of how the candle looked sitting in their home, how it smelled, and how the overall experience made them feel. Typically, the label is what they think about when they think of these things because it is your label that they stare at every day.

Here are some important things to remember:

- **Color Tips:**
  - o For label printing, CMYK values or Pantone Matching Values (PMS) are the best to go with, but a Hex code works as well.
  - o Make sure the colors are something your target audience would specifically appreciate. It might also be beneficial to study the science of colors and how they relate to emotions for this as well. You want your label color choice to be something that your target audience resonates with in a positive way.
  - o Most people choose colors that match their website to ensure that their branding is cohesive. However, you could come out with limited edition lines or other special candles that don't use your typical color scheme.
- **Font Tips:**
  - o The font is critical. Remember to keep your target audience in mind here as well. It must be eye-catching and easy to read. More than that, though, whoever creates your labels will need to know the instructions revolving around kerning, weight, and other things.

- **Sizing Tips:**
  - o Not only does the font have to be legible, but the entire design needs to be big enough that it's easily read from across the room.
  - o A good rule of thumb is to look at your candle straight on. Your label should cover the entirety of the front face of the candle container. Doing so will ensure it is legible to your customers and any potential new customers that see the candle from farther away.
- **Phrasing Tips:**
  - o Aside from the font type you choose, the words you choose are even more important. There is an endless combination of phrases and enticing words you can put on your candle labels but remember that most of the time, simplicity is the best option.
  - o You might decide that your logo plus a short description of the scent is enough for your label. Maybe you'll take it a step further and add a back label with a short paragraph description loaded with Call-To-Action (CTA) words that grab the reader's attention and make them more willing to buy your products.
  - o Come up with a few different design types and run them by trusted friends and professionals in the sales industry!
- **Imagery Tips:**
  - o Your logo is considered an image, and this is usually enough imagery for a candle label. However, some candles—typically those that

feature natural scents of lavender, eucalyptus, or another plant—will include imagery of the main scent included in the candle.

o Remember to keep things simple and uncluttered.

The great thing about candle making is that you rarely have any warnings or mandatory information to include on your labels. More often than not, candles have some of the more simplistic labels you'll see. Also, keep in mind that just because you created a label doesn't mean you have to keep it forever. Owning a business is a learning experience, and that goes for label creation as well. You will most likely look back six months from now and think to yourself, "What was I thinking with this label?!" That's okay!

You will likely have this thought a lot about your growing business. That is what it's all about. The most important thing is that you continue to learn and put in that work to make your business better and better. We are in an ever-changing market. Your target audience's needs are ever-changing, so your business will be ever-changing as well.

Remember, too, that there are professional designers out there that would love to help you create your label as well as your logo. If you know you aren't experienced in the design industry at all, this might be your best bet. However, if you are determined to learn, start by studying other successful candle-making companies. Look at their labels and packaging. Study where things are placed, how many words they use, the color scheme they chose, and if their labels are consistent across all of their candles.

Going off this same concept, think about how you can create labels and packaging that stand out from the crowd but are still practical for your candles. For instance, most soaps are wrapped in a paper label, and that's pretty much all they need for packaging. Most of the time, if you buy local, the owner will place the bar of soap in a small drawstring bag for you upon purchase, but you rarely ever see soap packaged in a rectangular-shaped tin can. Maybe your candles will take the tin can approach as means of standing out while still maintaining practicality.

Chapter 9: Protect Your Business: Knowing Laws and Having Insurance

Now, it's time for the really fun stuff: business laws and insurance protection. We have already spoken a bit about taxes and registering your business as an entity for tax purposes. This not only makes your business official, but it subjects you to various tax benefits, including tax write-offs for all things business-related. This may even include gas mileage in certain circumstances. We haven't touched much on the different laws set in place for candle-making businesses and whether or not insurance is something to consider.

Before you even think about selling your first candles, you are advised to speak with a business attorney in your area. The business attorney will have a complete list of legal advice for you to ensure you do everything by the book for your local county, state, and even federal purposes.

That said, there are a few things that are considered general public information where federal laws are concerned. This e-book is by no means considered expert legal advice. Rather, this chapter is specifically dedicated to general public legal advice. Below are some federal standards set in place that all candle-making businesses are expected to follow. Still, always consult with a legal professional before moving forward with your business.

The Laws for Selling Candles in the U.S.

Throughout the history of candle making, the world has seen a great shift from candles strictly being for functionality purposes to more of a decorative piece for the home that doubles as an air freshener. There are such beautifully crafted candles in the world that sometimes we forget that lighting one means you are inviting a fire risk into the home. You don't want your customers worrying about the safety of your candles, and the National Candle Association doesn't want to worry about it either.

In the late '90s, the world saw a rise in house fires directly resulting from candles. Some candles weren't placed in fire-safe areas, while others were exploding in their glass containers while families slept. The U.S. Consumer Product Safety Commission (CPSC) asked the National Candle Association to play a leading role in creating national standards for candlemakers in the U.S., which are the standards the nation still relies on today.

The standards were published via the ASTM International Standards Organization, and a complete list of standards and their descriptions can be found here:
https://www.astm.org/COMMIT/SUBCOMMIT/F1545.htm

We realize that these are standards made strictly for the U.S., but the rest of the world seemed to follow suit and created their own varying versions of these same standards for fire safety.

Below is a list of all of the standards, without their descriptions:

- The Cautionary Labeling Standard (ASTM F-2058)
- Fire-Safety Design Standard (ASTM F-2417)
- Heat Strength of Glass Containers Standard (ASTM F-2179)
- Candle Accessories Standard (ASTM F-2601)
- Standard Guide for Terminology Relating to Candles and Associated Accessory Items (ASTM F-1972)
- Standard Test Method for Collection and Analysis of Visible Emissions from Candles as They Burn (ASTM F-2326)

Aside from industry safety standards, which should be taken into the highest consideration, there are a few other legal considerations to be aware of.

Other Legal Considerations

Your creations and website are the lifeblood of your candle-making business. It is important to protect them from copyright issues and other negative outcomes. Again, be sure to consult with a business legal professional on these matters to ensure you have the most current information available for your state and county.

Still, below is some generally accepted information regarding trademarks and copyright, as well as website legalities.

Trademarks and Copyright

Investing in a trademark and copyright is one of the only ways to protect your business idea from being stolen. Without it, someone can get away with launching identical candles and get them copyrighted before you do. Once someone else copyrights them, you no longer can. That is why the sooner this is done, the better.

Many large candle manufacturers have their own fragrances and designs. Naturally, they trademark, patent, or copyright these things to protect them from other companies stealing their work. You don't have to be a large company to do this. If you created your own designs for your labels and packaging, be sure to have these copyrighted to ensure they stay yours and only yours. The same goes for any unique fragrances you come up with.

Once you acquire such legal paperwork, if you see another company selling products with your patented name, design, or fragrances, you are well within your rights to serve said company with a "cease and desist" notice. Once this notice is served, the company can no longer sell these products until the matter is closed or settled.

Website Legalities

As far as your website goes, there are a few legal things you should include on there as well, including:

- Your trademarks and copyright limitations
- Whether or not your prices are subject to change

- A disclaimer of warranties and liabilities
- A terms and conditions page

Typically, the terms and conditions page outlines all applicable laws and standards regarding candle making on a federal basis as well as a state and county basis. Including this in your site will give your customers peace of mind and protect you from legal issues down the line if an accident occurs with one of your candles in someone's home.

Is Insurance Necessary?

These aren't the only ways to protect yourself and your business from negative legal matters. You might also consider opting for an insurance policy for your business. As mentioned above, candles are beautiful works of art, but they can become a liability rather quickly. Where there is fire and glass, there is a need for insurance that not only protects you in the event of an accident, but your business in the event of an accident in the home of a customer.

Believe it or not, if someone accidentally drops your candle in their home and it breaks, you could be held liable. If the candle is lit when this happens, it will only make matters worse. Something like this would fall under third-party property damage, and more often than not, it is the business owner that foots the bill. It's an event like this that could cost you your dreams if you do not protect your business with an insurance policy.

In fact, there are two policies in particular that every candlemaker should have:

General Liability Insurance:

General Liability Insurance protects your business from physical risks like property damage and bodily injuries.

Professional Liability Insurance:

Professional Liability Insurance protects your business from more obscure things like any potential mistakes, errors, or omissions in your services/product.

A few other things you will usually find covered under these two policies are:

- **Defense Costs**
    - Anything of value damaged in the midst of the property damage, the insurance policy will cover.
- **Medical Coverage**
    - In the event that you or one of your customers gets injured by your product, the policy will cover it.

You might not think that Professional Liability Insurance coverage is as necessary as General, but it is. At the end of the day, you are only human, and humans make mistakes. It is always better to be safe than sorry, and you can typically get a slight discount for buying more than one policy anyway. Luckily, candle-making businesses usually don't need anything more than liability coverage, which does save you money compared to other types of businesses.

Some insurance companies will even allow you to pay by the month, the week, the day, or even the hour. Whatever suits your needs the most as a candlemaker, insurance companies will usually work with you.

Protecting yourself and your business is of the utmost importance. There is no point in doing all of the hard work you do if you don't protect yourself. There are way too many variables in life that could end up taking your business away from you. Of all things to budget, definitely include the above-stated things.

Chapter 10: Becoming a Business

We've talked about becoming a business in the eyes of the government via registering your businesses as an entity, but what does it truly mean to be a business owner in today's world? As mentioned previously, we live in an ever-changing world, especially where business is concerned. So what does it take to not only launch and sustain your business, but to remain relevant as well?

At the end of the day, it starts and ends with you. You are the owner, and if you aren't willing to go the extra mile, the chances of your business remaining a success diminish greatly. In a way, some might feel deterred by that statement. Truthfully, though, that is why a majority of businesses don't make it out of their first year. It is within that first year that you will face some of the hardest obstacles and longest workweeks of your entire life. This first year might extend a few years outward. The key is to remain resilient and with your eyes on the prize.

However, you tend to find out whether or not you are truly passionate about your career choice within the first year as well. From a strong and resilient mental state to remaining passionate about business and learning the ins and outs of your industry, you will live and breathe your business. Continue reading to learn some of the secrets behind remaining resilient and business hungry, as well as some Business 101 techniques for owning a business in today's world.

Starting a Successful Business 101

Some will tell you that it is imperative that you pay attention to the changing economic market and that launching a business in the midst of a recession is one of the worst things you can do. However, the best time to launch your business is when you are ready - when you feel the time is right and you have jumped through all the hoops to ensure that everything is in order.

But how?

How do you decide, "Okay, today is the day that I launch my first candle to the public"?

What if you don't have that large social media following that allows people to essentially launch a business and grow into a success seemingly overnight?

These are all important questions to answer, but of course, the answer itself is multi-faceted in nature. There is a list of things you must do before you are ready to launch, but one great thing that can help your initial launch is smart marketing and advertising. We will talk in great detail in the following chapter about branding your business and how to successfully market yourself. Once you have a nice marketing plan in order, you might have a good number of people interested in your product by the time the launch date comes around.

Either that or you can plan to launch without advertising beforehand. You might not sell as many things at first, but it will provide you with a little more time to sift through any errors and branding obstacles before you become a prominent name in the public eye. Typically, though, it is best to have a marketing plan in place before launching your first product.

The Basics of Business

We won't cover all of these in great detail here because they are covered in other sections of the e-book, but there are essential basics of business that everyone should be aware of before diving into the world of business. As a business owner, you will be responsible for most—if not all—of these things.

The essential basics of business include:

- Branding
- Marketing
- Sales Strategies
- Website Creation
- Social Media Marketing and Management
- Taxes and Accounting
- Financial Management
- Attracting Wholesalers
- Business Viability
- Workspace Cleanliness and Efficiency

Regardless of your level of expertise, there are resources and experts out there for you to learn from. Anything is possible with enough passion and determination to succeed. If you are serious about starting your business (you most likely are if you've made it this far in the e-book), then you will find a way to succeed in this industry.

The business skills that haven't been covered in other sections of the e-book are discussed in the section below. Aside from marketing and branding—those are things covered in the next chapter.

Business Skills All Business Owners Possess

In terms of business skills, as an owner, you have to be more of a jack-of-all-trades type of business person. You can't rely on a team of business professionals to do everything for you. If you did, you would be spending a large amount out of pocket before you ever launched anything, and your business wouldn't really feel like your business any longer.

It is always great to consult with other professionals in the same industry and in other industries, but at the end of the day, you want the big decisions to be left up to you. So your only option is to become as business savvy as possible.

Here are the key business skills that every business owner possesses:

Strategic Management

Strategic management is the process of setting objectives, analyzing the competition, internal organization, evaluating strategies, and ensuring those strategies are rolled out properly throughout the business. In other words, it is the initiative you take to ensure that your business plan comes into fruition as planned. More than that, though, it is the process of ensuring that all of your daily, weekly, monthly, and yearly goals are always met on time. It provides the overall direction of your business.

This is incredibly important for business owners because of how busy and hectic running a business really is. Running your business without a consistently updated strategic plan or objective is similar to trying to fill customer orders without an order sheet. It is nearly impossible. It also allows you to gain a competitive edge over others in the industry. Essentially, it is how you get ahead in the candle-making industry. If you aren't constantly logging your own efficiency and simultaneously analyzing the competition, you don't stand a chance against them.

Analyzing your competition is never a bad thing either. Everyone does it. Others are analyzing how you run your business. It is how the business world continuously improves to provide a better experience for the customer.

Basic Accounting

As far as tax accounting goes, your best bet is to leave that to the professionals. However, all business owners should have a basic understanding of accounting, in terms of which records to keep, the best way to organize and save them, and ensuring they get filed correctly.

There are also five basic accounting principles that all business owners should be aware of:

- **Revenue Recognition Principle:**
  - o The time when revenues are recorded through the income statement. If you are on an accrual basis, this allows your revenues to be recorded when the service was provided.
- **Cost Principle:**
  - o These are the records you keep of any expenses for the company. If you purchase a product from another company, record these costs immediately to keep your expenses in order. This also helps you maintain your set budget.
- **Matching Principle:**
  - o Ensure that your expenses match with your revenues recognized for that same accounting period. It is important to record these things in the same time period they were incurred. This is the true way to know how much you spend vs. how much you make during a given time period.
- **Full Disclosure Principle:**
  - o Always complete your financial statements to the letter. You don't want anything to be misleading. This also helps future clients or partners be made aware of all relevant information.
- **Objectivity Principle:**
  - o This should go without saying, but your accounting data should always be free of personal opinions. This is an area of your business that is strictly numbers to give you an accurate portrayal of the financial state of your

131

business. You also want to make sure all data is backed with evidence like receipts, vouchers, or invoices. Be sure to photocopy all evidence to have a digital copy for added convenience.

Financial Management

Financial management is anything and everything you can do to stay on top of your business's finances. This includes things like bookkeeping, projections, financial statements, and financing or loans. Without successful financial management, strategic management becomes ten times harder. You simply cannot reach your projected heights of success without solid financial management.

Get yourself into the habit of keeping every receipt and writing down every financial profit as well as expense. Financial management doesn't have to be boring and monotonous either. There are a few different websites and apps that can help you easily keep track of your finances. The trick is just to find what works best for you and try to turn it into a fun habit, because as long as you own a business, you will have to keep track of these things.

People Management

If you work for yourself and you don't hire any employees, your people management tasks will be a lot simpler than those that do. However, there's a chance in the beginning that you will hire a few different business professionals and other people to help you get certain things accomplished. The idea behind people management is that you are aware of their efficiency as well as morale.

You want their experience with your company to be as positive as possible because it sets the tone for your business. Not only that, but everyone that feels they've had a positive experience with your company will be more likely to tell other people about your products.

If you do hire employees, you'll want to be on top of organizing your team in a way that increases productivity. That said, you also want to be as flexible as possible with their lives and work schedules to keep that morale up, as mentioned above.

Sales

Sales in business are multi-faceted. In general terms, it is the transaction of money in exchange for ownership of your product. However, it also refers to your ability to land such a transaction. This is also where branding and marketing come into play. This is oftentimes one of the harder business skills to master because it takes a certain kind of personal skill as well.

There are some people out there that love to go out and attract new customers and can word things in a way that lands sales. Then there are those that prefer to go a different route and try to obtain more sales via online promotions and hiring social media influencers and things like that.

Regardless of how you do it, sales are what keeps your business alive. Without them, your business would continue to stay a hobby. As a business owner, you might go through waves where you get a large sum of sales and other waves where you barely sell anything. This is also why financial management is so important in business. You might not always have a steady flow of sales. However, as you continue to learn sales techniques, and the more you practice them, you will gradually learn what works for you and what doesn't.

Operations Management

Operations management goes hand-in-hand with people management and strategic management. This is how you obtain the most optimized business practices. When you first launch your business, you might think one way of operation is the most efficient for you, and it might be! However, it is crucial that you are always on top of your efficiency and productivity levels to ensure your operations are always fully optimized. No one wants to work harder than they have to, especially when they own their own business. Operations management has the ability to take some of the load off of your shoulders to free up more of your time while still putting out the same quantity and quality of work.

This also revolves around any suppliers and wholesalers you work with. The goal is to maintain happy, healthy relationships that are also as efficient as possible.

If you feel it will be too difficult to do all of these things on your own, you can hire employees to help you with these aspects of the business. Still, it would probably be cheaper in the long run for you to even enroll yourself in a business or sales course and try learning the ropes yourself. It would likely stall your launch date but would pay off in the end.

Managing Your Budget

Budgeting is extremely important for new businesses. It's extremely important for established businesses as well. So far, we've touched on things to include in your initial budget and how much it generally costs to launch a start-up. What we haven't covered is exactly how to manage that budget.

When you first decide you want to turn your dreams into reality and launch your first business, the excitement and creativity run wild. It can be easy to get lost in all the excitement and want to spend money on anything and everything to help achieve those goals. If you have a day job, you might have a little more wiggle room to expand your budget to incorporate all of the little things. However, most people do not. Therefore, you must be a little picky in the beginning to ensure you stay within your budget.

As a new business, you only want to purchase things that are necessities at that time. There are some things that might feel like you need them before you launch. In reality, they can wait until you sell a few candles and get a nice customer base before purchasing.

Below are tips to help you make these tough decisions so you can more wisely manage your budget:

Separate Personal Funds from Business Funds

To some, this might seem like a no-brainer. However, it is more common than you might think for new business owners to combine their personal and business funds, at least in the beginning. That said, launching your business and even prior to launch are both crucial budgeting times. When you have one bank account for your business and personal life, you make it unnecessarily hard on yourself to track money flowing in and out.

In turn, this can lead to overspending. It also leads to a misconception of how much money you are making and becomes increasingly harder to monitor and track profitability and spending down the line. Bank account statements are such a useful tool for tracking these sorts of things. Why have the unnecessary clutter of personal spending mixed in there when you could have two separate bank accounts to help monitor both sides of your life?

Even if you aren't required to have a business bank account just yet, it is wise to go ahead and open a separate checking account for your business. If you have to go to another bank to do so, it might prove to be even more beneficial to have entirely separate banks for your two accounts.

Monitor Your Spending

Learning to monitor your spending goes hand-in-hand with the basic accounting skills mentioned earlier in the chapter. If you aren't aware of how much you spend on a given day, week, or month, it becomes nearly impossible to monitor your budget. Misuse of funds is also a red flag that pops up when funds aren't properly managed.

Many business owners have multiple accounts for their business, including checking, savings, and even credit card accounts. When you first begin, you may only have a checking and potentially a credit account, but a savings account is extremely beneficial for businesses because it allows you the opportunity to prepare for unforeseen obstacles as well as business investments in the future.

A business credit card account is also extremely beneficial, especially in the beginning. It gives you the flexibility of buying things and paying for them a little later, as we all are well aware of by now. That said, just like with your personal credit card, you have to be careful not to overspend on your business credit card. It can get you into trouble with overspending if you aren't carefully monitoring your budget and can put you in a hole before you really get your feet off the ground - not to mention the fact that you also have personal bills and credits to pay for as well, so adding on business credit in the very beginning is risky.

Uncashed checks are another extremely important aspect to consider. If you are writing checks to anyone for your business, be sure to record this payment and subtract it from your spending whether or not it has been cashed already. Doing so will help you budget and ensure you aren't spending money that isn't there. The last thing you want to do is accrue overdraft fees before you even launch your business.

Time Your Purchases Wisely

That brings us to our next topic of timing your purchases out wisely according to your budget and monthly income. Being low on cash causes unnecessary stress that is easily avoidable by timing your purchases. A great way to ensure you stay on top of your cash flow is to pay all your bills before making any other purchases for your business that month.

You also don't want to bank on the money coming in and making purchases before you actually have that money in your account. The money may come later than you anticipated or not at all! It is a good rule of thumb to maintain a balance of a few hundred dollars at all times in your business checking account. This is not counting your potential savings account either. It is also best to have a few hundred on hand before spending any money because you always want to be prepared for surprise payments.

In other words, always leave room for human error. You are a human being that makes mistakes. It is wrong to put such pressure on yourself as ensuring you will never forget to write down a bill payment or some other payment type. Maintaining a cushion balance in your checking account assures you won't suffer too badly when these surprise payments occur.

Increase Revenue by Cutting Costs

Decrease expenses (as much as possible) and increase your income.

This is a concept that is relatively simple to grasp but might not seem realistic at first. You will obviously need to spend some money before you start acquiring an income from your business. That is why most people keep their day job until they feel they can securely support themselves with their business income.

If there is any way to increase your income to allow for more business expenses, do so. Whatever it takes to get good initial savings for your budget, do it!

However, once you begin selling your candles and your business starts to see an income, this concept becomes ever-important. In order to cut costs, you must be on top of your expenses. When you analyze your expenses, you will most likely find that you can scale back in a few areas in order to see a small increase in revenue. Monitoring your slow seasons is also important because it shows you when the best times to scale back are!

Maybe your current vendors are the issue as well. Something that worked for your business initially might not be so practical down the line. Be sure to stay informed of all the vendor options available to you and shop around for lower prices when need be.

Another great way to increase revenue is by offering promotions and discounts on your products, but we will get more into this in the next chapter.

Be Aware of Deadlines

Just to be clear, *bill* deadlines are what we are talking about here! Part of managing your budget is ensuring that all your bills are paid on time. When you miss a bill payment, the dreaded late fee ensues. One too many late fees not only puts you in a hole you could have avoided, but it hurts your credit as well.

No one wants bad credit, but bad business credit is one of the worst things to suffer from. It can be detrimental to your business and lead to your inability to acquire a business loan in the future. As a small business, you might not be worried about maintaining a business loan, but you never know what the future holds. You might find later on that a loan could help you get further ahead in your business.

It is best to always keep the option open. Not only that, but vendor relationships can suffer from bad business credit as well. All in all, it is just best to ensure that all your deadlines are met, and everything is always paid on time.

Accounts Payable vs. Accounts Receivable

You may or may not already be aware of the differences between accounts payable (AP) and accounts receivable (AR). These are both important considerations to remember while budgeting throughout the life of your business.

Accounts Payable

These are essentially payments you owe vendors. If your vendors allow you to pay in credit, this can be extremely beneficial when it comes to funding new projects. It gives you time to hopefully make money from those new projects before paying for the materials used. However, you still owe these companies money. In turn, this becomes a bill deadline you must be aware of. Missed vendor payments are frowned upon in the business world and could result in the loss of that vendor relationship.

Accounts Receivable

On the other hand, if you offer credit options for your customers (as a majority of businesses do nowadays), you could be looking at delays in receiving payment for your goods. These delays could be a month or longer depending on if the client pays on time. Not only do you have to stay on top of all of your accounts receivable, but there are ways to try to get your clients to pay their debts earlier.

Some business owners provide early payment discounts for those that pay their credits before the deadline. This will help you stay on top of accounts receivable and help you get your money sooner, which is just an added bonus!

Manage Your Inventory

Especially when you are first starting out, there really isn't a need for a large inventory. This is one area of the budget that business owners tend to overspend on in the beginning. It is so easy to get lost in all the available options and creative possibilities when it comes to making your first candles. That is why it is so important to create one line for candles (the simpler, the better) and stick to that for your initial launch. This will help you maintain an accurate inventory.

On the other side of things, managing your inventory comes down to timing your purchases as well. It is important to stay on top of the things you are running low on. You also want to remember that buying your inventory in bulk is always best! That said, you might buy more of one thing than anything else to ensure that you run out of supplies around the same time. However, you also want to make sure that all that is timed perfectly for when your bills are due to ensure there is enough money to cover all of your expenses.

The Importance of a Cash Reserve

This isn't necessarily as important if you haven't even launched your business yet. However, it is an important budgeting tip to know so you can stay on top of it when the time comes. Your cash reserve where your savings account comes into play.

Sometimes, unexpected things happen. Just like your personal life, it is important to have money saved up for those rainy days in your business life as well. Sure, you can use your credit card for scenarios like this, but you don't want to have to rely on your credit card solely. It is best to have a cash reserve in place to allow for peace of mind and cushion in those scenarios. You never know what will happen and how much it will cost.

With these eight budgeting tips, you can walk into the launch of your business with a head start on money management that will take you far in the future.

Personal Skills That Help in Business

You may not come from a line of business owners, but that doesn't mean you don't have the power to learn these skills entirely of your own volition. That said, every business owner also has the following set of personal skills that give them the ambition and determination to excel in the above-stated areas.

Passion

Passion is usually the first thing you felt and is the reason why you decided to turn your hobby into a business. And it is your passion that will allow your dreams to come true. Without passion, there would be no business anywhere. The entire reason anyone goes into business is that they have some sort of purpose. They want to achieve something or bring something to life. Sometimes that driving force is simply to make money, which is absolutely fine! After all, money is how the business world goes round.

Those that have another driving force behind their passion tend to get more out of their business as far as satisfaction is concerned. Not only that but when your passion comes from a genuine place, you tend to be more successful.

Persistence

Persistence is also a key quality in a business owner. When you launch your business, you will undoubtedly get some form of pushback. There will be obstacles you must overcome, and there will be things that don't go as planned. You must continue to push forward no matter what. There will be days when it seems you haven't any persistence left within you, and on those days, remember your passion. Remember why you started.

You don't want to be the person that pushed forward and pushed forward only to give up just before the finish line. Remember that the sun will shine once again, no matter how dark the skies seem right now. It is this kind of mindset that will keep your persistence thriving and allow you to continue on to those brighter days ahead.

Resilience

Resilience goes hand-in-hand with persistence. You must have tough skin in business. You may have heard this a time or two already. Prepare to get told no a lot by wholesalers and even customers. Prepare for the hard days ahead because you will experience them. It all comes with the joys of business.

Even so, those that are resilient are those that get to live out their dreams. There might come a time when you realize your original business plan isn't as effective as you once thought. You have to be willing to see this and understand that it isn't your sign to give up. Rather, it is your sign to keep a level head and figure something else out. Those with deep-driven passion and resilience are the ones that end up owning successful businesses.

Resourcefulness

Business owners are also 100% resourceful. This is probably their best quality. As mentioned above, when you own a business, you become a sort of jack-of-all-trades. You will do the work of ten people just to see your one dream come true. You will find the answer where you never thought to look. You will learn things you never thought possible, and you will experience things you never expected.

Having this quality will take you far, regardless of the path you choose in life. Be resourceful and soak up all that knowledge and experience like a sponge. The more you are passionate, persistent, and resilient to learn everything you can about your business and the industry, the more it'll pay off in the end.

Great Listeners

As a business owner, they say you should always try to have your finger on the pulse. In other words, you have to completely immerse yourself in your craft and the industry as a whole. Part of this immersion means having your ears on the pulse as well. All of the successful business owners are great listeners. They listen to their employees (if any), their customers, their partners, friends, and family—and their competition.

When you live your life completely immersed in your business, it becomes second nature to hear things that can benefit your business in many different ways. Things that help steer you in the right direction and things that can even serve as warnings you might be headed in the wrong direction.

One characteristic of every great listener is that they can listen without their pride or ego getting in the way. This can be hard when someone is trying to give you constructive criticism about your business. After all, it is something you put your heart and soul into, so it's understandable if you don't like hearing negative comments from people. However, if you can try to listen as if the business isn't your own, it will help you listen from an objective standpoint rather than a subjective one.

Objectivity

Speaking of objectivity, it is a lot harder to succeed as a business owner if you aren't willing to look at your business from an objective standpoint, regardless of what the situation is. Whether you are listening to feedback from a fellow peer or customer, or you are analyzing business efficiency, objectivity is key.

That said, you must also be ever-present in all aspects of your business. If you aren't, it becomes even harder to remain objective. Living in the past or future causes your mind to dream up scenarios that might not necessarily be truthful. In turn, objectivity is impossible. Maintaining an objective mindset will also ensure you are at your most creative. It is when we allow superficial tendencies to cloud our minds that creativity becomes stifled. It also becomes harder to make rational business decisions in a superficial mindset.

Above all else, remember that you are human. Yes, a great business owner can embody all of the above-listed characteristics, but that doesn't mean they come naturally to you. You might feel as though you do not embody these characteristics all at once either. This is perfectly normal and absolutely okay.

Allow yourself grace. Be patient with yourself and be patient with your business. The chances of turning into an overnight success are extremely slim, and that is just the honest truth. Successful businesses take work, long and tiring hours, and many gruesomely late evenings. Keep these characteristics in mind, but more so as tips to remember and work toward. They will help you on your path to achieving greatness.

Chapter 11: Now It's Time to Market Your Business

Mustering up the courage to start your own business is difficult enough. Sticking with that business through thick and thin is even harder, but learning how to effectively market that business and promote it in a way that is sustainable to your growth and success is a completely different ball game. This is especially true for those that don't have any experience in the business or marketing industry. If this is you, you might feel as though you've jumped into the deep end after only one swimming lesson.

The following chapter is set out to help you become a little more aware of the marketing world and different tips with tricks to catapult your business to where you want it to be. By the end, you will have the basic skills necessary to market your business in a professional manner, which will naturally instill confidence in yourself and your business.

Getting to Know Your Customers

Regardless of what you are selling, your customers are always your number one priority, especially when promoting your business. We have touched on what a target audience is and understanding your demographic in previous chapters, but now we will uncover how that pertains to marketing.

How Do You Advertise to Your Demographic?

When targeting your demographic, there are a few things to remember. Let's go over them now as a refresher:

• Age
• Pronoun usage
• Geography
• Spending behavior
• Median annual income
• Where they spend their free time
• Other things that consume their attention

If you are going to reach this target audience, you first have to analyze your customer base to ensure you are targeting the right crowd. It is important to revisit this often. Your target audience isn't likely to change much, but it can. You always want to make sure your promotions are tailored toward your most recent and specific audience.

You must then create content that is useful and relevant to that audience type. That is the tricky part. The only way you can create meaningful and relevant content is if you are immersed in what your target audience enjoys, where and how they spend their free time, and so forth. Being familiar with other trending topics for that particular demographic is extremely beneficial as well. Look to see how other businesses in other industries target the same demographic.

There are three major ways to market your business that seem to appeal to any demographic. These three marketing tactics include:

- **Video Marketing:**
    - o Yes, photos are great and all, but videos provide more detail. It's just that simple. Customers want to see the product being used. They want the full effect before they purchase. They want to know exactly what they are buying.
- **Social Media Marketing:**
    - o Video marketing is prominent in social media marketing. However, there are other avenues granted within social media marketing that video marketing alone cannot provide. You gain access to the broadest audience possible, for one. There are also different ways to connect with customers via live chats, stories, photos, etc.
- **Blog Marketing:**
    - o Writing quality blogs that are SEO optimized is one of the quickest ways to get your website and merchandise visible on Google and other search engines. Depending on what you write about, you can easily get your target audience hooked from a few thought-out pieces.

Social media marketing is also great because if you don't have a large following there, you can hire a few influencers to promote your products to boost sales. The great thing about social media and influencers is that it isn't a place solely for the younger generation anymore. There are influencers for every demographic. In fact, influencer marketing is so effective that of the 80% of marketers that find influencer marketing to be effective, 71% of them find the traffic to be better than their other sources of marketing.

Choosing to market through influencers also increases your chance of expanding your reach and broadening your target audience.

Targeted Advertising

This is another area where social media and Google have the upper hand over other traditional forms of advertising. Google ads and social media ads like those on Facebook all have advanced options to help you better target your audience via filling out your preferred demographics, location, and interests of your audience. The ads will then show up for users that fall under these options, thus being more likely to be interested in and buy your product.

Building a Social Media Platform, Web Presence, and Email Marketing Campaign

We've talked a little about the different ways you can market your company, but now let's dive a little deeper and talk about various things you can do to make these different marketing strategies work for you. There are three major areas you should be spending most of your energy when it comes to marketing: building your social media platform, improving website visibility, and launching an email marketing campaign. This is the trifecta that, in 2021, will help you remain relevant and grow a successful business.

Building Your Social Media Platform

As mentioned, social media is by far the most useful marketing tool today. It certainly isn't the only marketing effort you should pursue, but it is a good idea to put most of your energy into building your platform before worrying too much about your web presence and email marketing. Those two things will come to you a lot easier once you have a solid social platform.

That said, you do not need millions of followers to be successful. At the beginning of social media marketing, it was thought that if your business didn't have millions of followers, you weren't successful. That simply isn't the case anymore. Especially as a small business, you can be wildly successful with as little as 5,000 followers. In fact, as that follower count gets higher, your business might not be so 'small' anymore and might force you to hire on more help. This may seem like the ultimate goal for everyone, but some people prefer to keep their business small and their customer base familiar.

Before you can begin building your social media platform, you must first decide which platforms work best for you and your business.

Below is a list of some of the more popular platforms to choose from in 2021:

• TikTok
• Facebook
• Instagram
• Twitter
• YouTube

• Pinterest

You will want to choose at least three of these social platforms to create content. The more, the better, but you also have to make sure you put out quality content suited for each platform. That is why it is recommended to focus on three platforms rather than all of them. For candle-making businesses, it is best to choose platforms that work well with photos and video. You might not need a YouTube channel, but if you feel like producing "how-to" videos, YouTube is a great platform to invest in. Other than that, TikTok, Facebook, Instagram, and maybe Pinterest are all great places to invest your time as a candle-making business owner.

TikTok

TikTok is by far the fastest growing social media platform today and is currently the easiest place to build a large following rather quickly. That's right, we said TikTok. For some, TikTok might feel like foreign territory because the younger generation seemed to take over the app. In reality, it is thanks to the younger generation that this platform is now popular for nearly any age group and nearly any niche.

More and more businesses are creating TikTok accounts to promote their products. It is also a great way for your customers to get a more behind-the-scenes feel of who makes their products. Unlike Instagram, the TikTok world doesn't expect you to be all done up and have beautiful content. Contrarily, most of the users tend to be drawn to the accounts that produce raw, unfiltered content; and the funnier and more original, the better.

Facebook and Instagram

Facebook is one of the oldest social media platforms that is still wildly popular today. TikTok is a great platform to be present on because of the trending aspect, but Facebook is where you can really home in on advertising. Not only that, but a few years ago, Facebook bought Instagram, so now those same advertisements will post directly to your Instagram platform as well. That is why it is great to have both. Instagram is a perfect place for a candle-making company. You can show off beautiful content and reach thousands, if not millions of users with one advertisement, via the two platforms.

Pinterest

Pinterest isn't meant for every business, but a candle-making business can go far on this platform. Those "how-to" videos we mentioned would also go great on Pinterest. You can even cross-post your Instagram content to this platform as well and expect it to translate beautifully.

Once you have decided which platforms you will work to build, next you will want to begin brainstorming content ideas and an overall theme for each platform. Bear in mind that the theme is likely to change with the different seasons of your business, but you still want to have a basic overall theme in mind for the launch of your social media business persona.

You also have to remember that your business accounts will take a lot more attention than your personal social media accounts. Obviously, if you have a following already built on your personal accounts, don't shy away from promoting your business via this platform. However, it's important to consider just how much time it will take to create meaningful content for your business account on each platform.

This is also where time management comes into play. Buy yourself a planner or set up a Google calendar to help you organize which days you will create content and which days you will create candles. Laying out your schedule will help you manage your time more wisely and not get overwhelmed by the workload.

Utilize Content Calendar Apps

Speaking of scheduling out your time, there are also numerous different content calendar apps that will automatically upload your content at the time you schedule. This makes business social media use a breeze. You can create as many posts as you want to at a time. Simply design the post, write a meaningful caption, and schedule the time you want the post to drop. The app will do the rest. These apps are also great for giving you a visual of what your timeline will look like when all the posts have dropped.

Cohesiveness is important in business and important on social media. You want your timeline to flow beautifully. Doing so will keep the audience engaged when they click on your profile. Before they know it, they will find themselves months down your timeline looking at your content.

Advertising on Social Media

We've already touched on this once and how important it is for targeting your audience and promoting only to those that are already interested in products similar to those that you sell. It's equally as important to understand that as the world of marketing becomes increasingly more social media-based and focused. This also means that paying for those advertisements has only seemed to increase over recent years.

Consistent advertising is better than trying to reach a vast number of people in a small amount of time too. It is also best to have a specific focal point in mind for your advertisements. People are tempted to spend money to advertise their stories. They want the world to know what their business is and why they started it. This is great, but you are likely to lose reader interest rather quickly if it doesn't have something that directly relates to them.

In other words, advertise one of your latest products and sprinkle in bits and pieces of your story along with it. You can even include a check-out option directly in your advertisements now. We will talk more about this in the sections below.

Improving Your Website Visibility

Building and improving your website visibility is another extremely important aspect of marketing your business. Building your social media presence will inevitably help your website's visibility as well. That is why it is a good idea to have your website created and launched when you launch your business social media accounts or soon after. This will help promote your cohesiveness and professionalism. If your followers don't have anywhere to go to look at your products, they are less likely to stick around for the long haul.

Etsy and Poshmark, as well as Facebook Marketplace and even Amazon, are great places to try and sell your products alongside your website. It might seem like a lot of work at first, so this might be a goal you set once your business is a little more established. Nonetheless, creating seller accounts on all of these different sites will help you reach a broader clientele and thus sell more products. It is a little harder to keep track of all of your sales if they are in numerous places. You might want to dedicate a select number of products to sell on each site, so you are certain that you don't oversell an item.

Social media and other seller websites aren't the only ways to promote your website/products, though. You can also create a blog for your website. Being familiar with Search Engine Optimization (SEO) is the best way to create blog posts that naturally rank high on Google search. Those that aren't familiar with the blogging world or SEO can easily find freelance writers to help them create their blogs. Blogs that rank high on Google mean more readers on your site and potentially buying your candles!

Later on down the line, you can even create a forum on your website. Forums are wonderful for traffic flow and keeping people on your website longer! They are also great for connecting with your customers and building that relationship that matters so much to them. Of course, it might be best to hold off on this until you have a solid customer base under your belt and a consistent flow of viewer traffic on your website. Regardless, this is just another option to help you promote your business.

You can always pay for Google ads as well. These ads can even be the same ads you run on Facebook and other social platforms. The only difference is your ad will appear across Google and reach more people. Even if viewers don't buy products directly from the ad, they will be familiar with your website and what you have to offer. They will most likely sign up for your email list as well to help them remember your site when they do want to purchase candles.

Just remember, marketing is important but is nothing without a professional, user-friendly website. Take your time creating your website. It is the face of your brand and will be the one thing people remember most about your business, other than your candles. Make it your own, and try your best to ensure it is all cohesive and follows the general theme and persona you have in mind for your business.

Launching an Email Marketing Campaign

Creating an email list is one of the easiest marketing tools there is. It isn't something you even have to promote. It is something that happens naturally as you promote your business in other areas, including social media. All you have to do is create a space on your website for visitors to sign up for your email list. If you've noticed, many people choose to place this at the bottom of one or all of the pages on their website. Others may even include a pop-up that appears when the user initially visits the site.

After that, your other marketing and promotional tactics will do the rest. Once you have acquired a decent email list, you can begin preparing your first email marketing campaign. You can even hire a freelancer to create this campaign for you if you don't have the time or feel a little clueless about where to begin. There are also free platforms that walk you through the design process to help you create campaigns on your own!

Where to Begin

For your first email, it is always great to welcome those that have joined and thank them for their support. You might even dedicate the email to telling them a bit about yourself and giving them a little sneak peek inside your workspace and what your daily work schedule looks like.

Remember, those that join the email list can be considered your loyal customers. They are the ones that have seen something they like about your company, and they are interested in learning more about what you have to say, as well as possibly benefiting from a few email promotional deals, A.K.A. secret discount codes only available to them.

Another great way to start is by launching a monthly newsletter. Maybe your first newsletter covers the simple things mentioned above! Once your email list begins to grow, you might try sending out that same monthly newsletter twice a month. You'll still be creating one newsletter a month but sending it out twice. This just ensures that everyone gets a chance at reading it and keeps your business in mind.

Other Ways to Market Your Business

Online is by far the most efficient way to market a business in today's world. However, it isn't the only way. Word-of-mouth is one of the oldest and truest forms of marketing and is still effective in its own right. It shouldn't be your only form of marketing by any means, but a business owner that mentions their business in casual conversation is a business owner dedicated to his/her business.

This simple method of word-of-mouth can spread like wildfire. Similarly, when you create quality products that your customers love, they are more likely to tell their friends about your business. On top of that, if the customer experience is great, that will increase the chances of them telling a friend even more!

Aside from good 'ole fashion word-of-mouth, there are a few other classic ways to help market your business. Some of these in-person marketing tactics include:

• Attending local events like markets and fairs
• Leaving business cards in other brick and mortar businesses
• Printing flyers
• Paying for ads in the local paper
• Hosting candle-making classes

As a small business owner, promoting your business locally will help you build those personal relationships that are so crucial in business. Especially when you are first starting out, having your local community on your side will help you go far in the Internet world as well. If you think about it, almost everyone uses social media today. So, in building those business relationships with the people that have known you the longest, they are more likely to share your business on their platforms as well.

As a business owner, even when you aren't working, you are always advertising, even when you aren't talking about your business! Those that see you as a business owner will remember how you treated them during work and outside of work. Being someone that people can trust and be inspired by will take you far regardless of your industry or your marketing plan.

The One-Page Template for Success

The one-page template for success is a template you can follow to create advertisements that are sure to have a solid turnaround. At the end of the day, if you combine this template with powerful sales and action words, you will easily draw in your customers, and they will be checking out before they know it.

Below is a basic layout of what the template should look like:

- Headline
- Lead
- Story
- Pitch
- Evidence
- Offer
- Close

The most important part of following this template is that you include these seven steps in the order they are presented above. This is a formula proven to work time and time again for converting viewers into customers. For a more in-depth description of this template, check out the info at try.samcart.com/1-page-blueprint-free.

How Are You Unique?

Think back to why you wanted to start your business and the persona you want your business to give off. Any specific details about the quality of your products, the artistic value, and anything else that makes your business stand out should be at the forefront of your marketing plan.

Start by making a list to help you organize the exact characteristics you want to convey to your audience, some of which may include:

• The wax quality
• Your variety of scents available
• Color variety
• Sculpture pillar candles
• Sustainability
• Long-lasting wick and wax

Use these characteristics to your advantage. If it's your core values and environmentally friendly products and packaging that makes you stand out, use your advertisements to showcase just how environmentally friendly your products really are. And remember, great video goes a long way in today's world.

Identify Your Peak Sales Periods for Specific Scents

Having a separate bank account for your business starts to pay off when you want to find out exactly when your busy season is and which scents sell the most during those periods. You want to capitalize on the busy season as much as possible. Your bank statements will give you an idea of when more payments come in as well as when you usually restock your inventory. Your website will show you who is buying what and how much they are buying, so you can get a clear idea of which candles are selling and which aren't.

Obviously, in the beginning, you will most likely only launch with a single line of candles. Still, you want to analyze how well these candles are doing and if it is worth it to continue the line while creating a new one. Chances are, you will continue your first line until you come up with a few more lines of candles that eventually outperform the original. You want to think that you will get better over time and create more candles your customers enjoy, so thinking of one day discontinuing your original line is actually a great goal to have.

That said, here are a few examples of which scents typically do well during each of the four seasons:

- **Spring:**
  - Floral scents like lilac, jasmine, magnolias, lemongrass, honeysuckle, lavender, and apple and cherry blossom.
- **Summer:**
  - Fresh scents like citrus, coconut, peach, linens, watermelon, sea salt, citronella, aloe, and even

sandalwood (which is also a great scent during the Fall and Winter).

- **Fall:**
  - o Fresh scents but also more spices than Summer scents, like pumpkin spice, sage, eucalyptus, amber, brown sugar, cedar, apple, and cinnamon.
- **Winter:**
  - o Spices paired with warmer woody scents, like cinnamon, vanilla, chestnut, sandalwood, peppermint, nutmeg, birch, sugar cookie, and maple.

Don't forget about limited edition holiday scents as well. Holiday scents always do well in sales, especially during the winter months.

Your customers will love to see how versatile you can get with your scent combinations. They want to know that they can count on you and your candles regardless of the season.

Contrary to popular belief, customers tend to be extremely loyal to the brands they love, even with their candles. Yes, there are some days when picking up a candle at the local grocery store is easy and convenient. However, when you find a candle you love from a small business, you are likely to continue to try their candles in the future. Customers like to know the person behind the candle, too, so don't be afraid to tell your story and how you got started with candle making and scent creations. Don't be afraid to list which candles are your personal favorites and why!

What to Do During the Slow Months

Just because you have identified your peak sales months and the scents that accompany those sales doesn't mean you shouldn't pay attention to your slow months. In fact, the opposite is more true. Don't get me wrong, you absolutely want to capitalize on your busy months, but it is just as important to pay attention to the slow months and which scents still sell during those periods.

Don't be afraid to advertise during these months as well. Always focus on the products that sell year-round, but focus on a couple of other scents that sell specifically during the slow seasons. Push your marketing toward these scents during the slow months and try marketing them even more than you do during your busy months.

You can even try making a few special marketing points during your slow seasons that you don't normally do, including things like:

• Email list discounts
• Gift pack promotions
• Keep track of email list birthdays and send a free gift
• Random holidays, like National Donut Day, can be great to promote sweet scents
• Be sure to double up on your social media presence during these times

Poor marketing is detrimental to the livelihood of your entire business. You can have the best idea on earth, but a poor marketing plan could leave you bankrupt. Similarly, there are businesses that get away with selling less than quality products and grow a successful business solely because of their marketing plan.

It is a good idea to invest much of your time learning how to properly and efficiently market your business. As much time as you spend coming up with and creating your candles, if you spend an equal amount of time on your marketing plan, you will learn quickly the things that work for your business and the things that don't.

As always, be sure to check out your competition as well. Look at established candle-making companies, businesses new to the scene, nationwide and international businesses, and local shops as well. There is a lot to learn about business and marketing today simply by analyzing your competitors.

In the next chapter, we will cover how to maintain and continue to grow a business for long-term success.

Chapter 12: Long-Term Success

Thinking about the long-term tends to be what scares new and future business owners the most. No one wants to spend time and money on a project that doesn't have the ability to make it in the long run. In short, no one wants to waste their time. It is always good to be thinking of your five and ten-year plans early on. That said, it might be a little early to go into immense detail about your plan, so we have included a generalized list for you to follow to make sure you reach all of your goals and in a timely manner.

Pay Attention to the Industry

When you run your own business, it's easy to get stuck in the day-to-day. Even if you still are working full-time somewhere else, most—if not all—of your free time is spent working on your business, researching for your business, or thinking about your business. In turn, you become so hyper-focused on your own business and how to make it better that you might forget about the rest of the industry, including your competition. It's no shock that the candle-making industry is a competitive field, even just in the small business sphere.

Rather than letting this intimidate you, use it to your advantage when it comes to planning for your long-term success. Remember how we mentioned earlier in the book about the importance of keeping your finger on the pulse of the industry? This extends to all aspects of your business, especially your long-term goals. Never stop learning about your industry. Never stop learning about your competitors. Look to those you perceive to be more successful than you. And when you see your own success, don't forget to pay attention to all the new and up-and-coming candle-making shops. These types of shops will give you insight into the successful shops that others simply cannot.

It's also important to note that just because you keep a watchful eye on your competitors doesn't mean you have to do it "their way." You started your own business so you could show *your* gifts to the world. However, don't be afraid to take some pointers and make them your own. That is what it's all about, which brings us to the next point.

Don't Reinvent the Wheel

This phrase can be taken two different ways. For starters, in the candle-making industry (and any other industry), there are a set of unspoken rules. These rules tend to revolve around what works and what doesn't. Candles have been around for centuries. Chances are, you most likely aren't going to come up with something that hasn't already been done.

For some, this can sometimes be a depressing comment. However, statistically, it seems to be true. Now, that doesn't mean it's impossible. There is absolutely room for innovative candles in the industry. Maybe you have an idea in mind already. Take that idea and run with it!

Still, it is unrealistic to think that every candle-making business or shop will create a type of candle or even a scent combination that hasn't already been done before. Therefore, use that certainty to your advantage. This is really when industry research comes into play. Study the numbers. See which types of candles and combinations seem to work best for others and at what time of year. Not only that, but check out different business personas, mission statements, and even marketing plans and modify them to work well for your business's ideals and mission.

Second, when it comes time to create a new line of candles, don't reinvent the wheel. In other words, stick with what you know and with what has been working. It is better to create cohesive synergies within your different products. This will help your customers identify with your branding. Otherwise, you run the risk of people not understanding your main persona, or worse, they might see the new products and pass them up because they don't ring true to your original output. The idea is to keep costs as low as possible, so you don't have to worry about much overhead.

Keep Money in Perspective

We've already talked about money management in previous chapters, but it is just as important when considering the future of your business. If you are trying to grow and scale your business, it's crucial to put some money back into your business. You can't grow if you don't make room for yourself to do so.

It's a good idea to always get your must-haves paid for first. All of your expenses must be in order. Only dip into your savings account to reinvest in your business, and even then, you don't ever want to completely drain that account. It's always important to have cash set aside for a rainy day.

If you feel you are having trouble making a profit at your business, you will need to reevaluate a few things. You must be willing to look at your work from an objective standpoint. It's also crucial to pay attention to the feedback you receive. If something isn't working, the public won't be afraid to tell you. Not only that, but expenses could be playing a large role in your success as well. As a small business, it is always better to have the least amount of expenses possible.

If that still doesn't work, try revisiting your marketing plan. Pay attention to what your customers are buying. How many products do they tend to buy at one time? If the answer is only one candle, try to focus your marketing efforts on upselling your current customers. Maybe consider adding a loyalty program to your site. Loyalty programs are a great incentive for customers to buy more. People love to receive points toward free items, especially to their favorite shops.

Be Willing to Pivot

It is all too common for people to have a certain vision in mind for their business that ends up looking entirely different when it's all said and done. The sad truth is that the professionals that aren't willing to see this for their own business tend to go under before ever creating real success. In fact, an overwhelming 90% of start-up businesses fail, and an inability to look at the business from an outside perspective and change the parts that are failing is the biggest reason.

At the end of the day, ego and pride tend to get in the way for some people. They have put their heart and soul into creating a vision they saw in their head. A vision they spend countless hours researching and developing only to find that it doesn't quite translate the way they hoped it would.

To clarify, pivoting doesn't mean you have to drop your candle-making business idea altogether. The idea behind this is that you can tweak a few things within your existing business plan to help your main point translate more fluidly to the public.

Below are a few signs that it might be time to pivot your business idea:

- You are always playing catch-up on bills.
- You always feel a step behind your competition.
- You seem to have hit a plateau.
- One item gets all the traction.
- You put more work in for little response.
- Maybe your ideals and perspective have changed.

If you have a successful business and you still want to pivot because of a personal perspective change, that is okay too! At the end of the day, it is your business, and your loyal customers will be respectful of your creative shift. That is the beauty of entering the artistic realm of business. Your customers are likely to not only understand your need for a creative shift but be on board with it wholeheartedly.

Pivoting is never something to fear. If anything, it gives your business another chance at success. Maybe only being a candle business isn't your calling. Maybe you are meant to add more diversity to your products. It still might be a good idea to consult with a business professional before doing so, especially if you already have yourself established and have received great feedback. Sometimes it is best to slowly introduce new products while still creating your most popular products. And if these new products are still somehow cohesive to your original successful products, even better!

Every Relationship Matters

Every person you come in contact with matters. When you are self-employed, it is crucial that you always have your best foot forward when meeting new people. You never know when you will meet someone that can help take you further in your career. Just because you are self-employed doesn't mean you have to be at it entirely on your own. This is just another reason why owning your own business can be so tiresome, especially when you are trying to grow that business.

You never know when you might meet a random stranger at the gas station who turns out to be one of your greatest business mentors. That is also why you always want to put yourself out there. Allow yourself the freedom to step outside of the studio every now and then. That is the only way you'll have a shot at meeting someone that could potentially have such an impact on the outcome of your business.

Have Fun at Work

Whether it is just you or you have hired a small staff of helpers, it is important that work is an enjoyable place to be for everyone. You can't expect yourself to get productive work done if you dread going to work every day. Just because your hobby is now your job doesn't mean it has to be boring and suck the life out of you. Most likely, one of your main reasons for wanting to start your own business has to do with the fact that you haven't liked your previous day jobs, for whatever reason.

Take what you've learned from all of those negative times to try and make your workspace the exact opposite. After all, it is your business. You should feel like you have the creative freedom to do whatever you want while at work.

Time management and workplace flexibility go hand-in-hand. When you are on top of your work schedule, it is easier to have a fun work environment. Successful time management skills lead to less stressful deadlines, which in turn lead to more free time. That will inevitably make work more fun for you.

In terms of having a fun work environment while you are creating projects, here are a few ideas:

- Work outside or in a random coffee shop on days when you are mostly doing planning and crunching numbers.
- Play music!
- A workspace with a nice view is always best.

If you have a few staffed workers, here are some fun ideas:

- Incentives for creating excellent candles in a timely manner.

- The ability to have a flexible work schedule within certain deadlines.
- Classic team-building days outside of the studio.

It's proven that activities like the above mentioned help improve morale and get everyone—including yourself—to work more efficiently. It is when we work people nonstop with zero rewards that they quickly become burnt out and quit. Make sure your work environment is a place you not only want to work at, but your customers would love to work at as well.

Never Stop Innovating

This may seem like a no-brainer, but innovation is necessary to have successful growth in your business. The thing about innovation is that it never stops. The moment you come up with a new idea and begin brainstorming ideas to turn it into reality, you should be thinking of another new idea. It is recommended to have weekly innovation meetings for your business.

It is always best to have these meetings with other people because brainstorming ideas alone isn't nearly as effective. Like they always say, "more heads are better than one."

Just because you have a popular product now doesn't mean that product will automatically be popular forever. However, when a once-popular product is no longer so, that doesn't mean you have to get rid of it altogether. That's also where innovation comes in, with a mix of slight pivoting. It might only take a few tweaks within the product's design or marketing plan to get it to rank high on your site once again.

Innovation is important in all aspects of your business, not just design and product creation. It might be necessary to brainstorm different marketing plans often. The business world is constantly changing. What works today quite literally might not work tomorrow. Try meeting up with marketing experts consistently to make sure your current marketing plan is modified for success in the current business climate.

If you have staffed workers or you have innovation meetings with outside business professionals, don't be afraid to take their ideas and run with them! Even if the idea seems ludicrous at first, it might just be the 180 your business needs to stay relevant in the ever-changing market. Contrarily, you might go months with consistent innovation meetings and not come up with anything. That is why it is so important to have consistent meetings. A missed meeting is a missed opportunity.

Consistently Revisit Your Long-Term Plan

Lastly, long-term business plans aren't a one-and-done type of thing. It also isn't something that you create and then put away until the five years go by. If you create a business plan and then never take the time to look at it and make sure you are on track, there is a good chance you will fall off track. The same goes for your long-term plan.

And because it is a long-term plan, you must also make the necessary revisions to ensure your long-term plan remains relevant throughout the years. That's the thing with long-term plans. They are usually five or even ten-year plans. To think that the plan you make today will be the exact plan you follow through with is absurd. Don't put so much pressure on yourself to create the perfect plan now.

All it takes is an essentially skeletal outline of what you plan to accomplish. Then, throughout the years, you can fill in the blanks with all of the details.

You can also use this e-book to help keep you on track! The first time you read this through, you might not even have a business yet. More realistically, you probably just have the idea to turn your hobby into a business. Therefore, thinking about the long-term might not even be in your wheelhouse at the moment, and that is perfectly okay. In fact, most people in that position won't be thinking about the long-term of their business until long after the launch of their business.

Still, it is great to have this information handy to you when it comes time to start planning. Everyone's long-term business plan will look different and will change a lot. Once you have created your original business plan, your long-term business plan will come more naturally to you. Keep all of the previously mentioned tips in mind, and be ready to call in other professionals for advice when needed.

Conclusion

Starting your own business is nerve-racking, to say the least. It's not something you can decide one day and then accomplish the next. It takes careful consideration and many hours of planning and research to launch a successful business in today's economy. Before you get started, it's also important to know the history of candle making, alongside all of the different types of candles, waxes, and wicks that are used today. You will also need to know what type of containers are best for candle making because you don't want an insurance liability on your hands.

Not to mention the fact that you are taking something you love to do and trying to make money at it. This always sounds ideal in the beginning, but for some, their hobby should have stayed a hobby. Once they add the business side to it all, they start to realize that they enjoyed the activity a lot more when it was just a hobby and didn't have all the stresses of business attached to it.

Perhaps the hardest part of turning your hobby into a business is the business side of it all, at least for most people. It all starts with the business plan, and this tends to be the fun part. This is where all of the brainstorming and planning happen and when you decide what your business persona will be along with your color schemes, logo, and probably even your branding as well.

Once your business launches, that's when the real fun starts. You are forced to come up with a solid marketing plan while simultaneously watching your revenue and expenses to ensure you aren't overspending and you are staying on budget. Especially in the first year, it is important to stay on top of your budget to make sure you always have enough money to pay all of your business bills and still be able to invest back into your dreams.

The road to success is long, and most of the time, it isn't paved. You must do the work to create your own roads that will take you to where you want to be. And sometimes, that work means taking time to relax and let yourself breathe. As a business owner, you must always take care of yourself first if you want to give your all to your business.

With the conclusion of this e-book, the hope is that you have learned a little something but, more importantly, you felt even the slightest spark of inspiration. Candle making can be extremely rewarding. You can one day have a self-sustaining business that allows you to fully quit your day job and continue building your dreams. This e-book is proof that there is a way to get you to where you want to be. If you want something, don't let anything stand in your way. You are the vehicle that will drive your dreams into a profitable reality.

Above all else, we would like to thank you for being here. There are so many different avenues you can take with your candle-making journey, and we are happy you chose this path to help get you started.

Now it's time to put what you've learned to good use and continue learning as you begin creating your first line of candles! We can't wait to see where your dreams take you!

References

https://candles.org/history/#:~:text=Paraffin%20wax%20
was%20introduced%20in,from%20petroleum%20and%20ref
ine%20it.

https://www.thomasnet.com/articles/top-suppliers/private-
label-candle-manufacturers-suppliers/

https://realsoycandles.com/blogs/news/history-of-candles-
and-candle-traditions

https://fraendi.com/blogs/blog/what-are-the-different-
types-of-wicks-you-can-use-to-make-a-candle

https://www.luxdeco.com/blogs/styleguide/luxury-candle-
buying-guide

https://www.homestratosphere.com/types-of-candles/

https://candles.lovetoknow.com/Candle_Making_Scent_En
hancements

https://www.lifenreflection.com/how-to-choose-the-best-
candle-scents/

https://www.businessnewsdaily.com/7456-workspace-
design-productivity.html

https://smallbusiness.chron.com/buy-building-business-42558.html

https://www.score.org/blog/how-hard-small-business-owners-work

https://startingyourbusiness.com/how-to-start-a-candle-making-business/

https://99designs.com/blog/tips/ultimate-guide-to-product-packaging-design/

https://www.bill.com/blog/business-101-5-essentials-starting-successful-business

https://www.patriotsoftware.com/blog/accounting/what-are-accounts-payable/